Aging in British Columbia

Burden or Benefit?

Herbert C. Northcott and P. Jane Milliken

Detselig Enterprises Ltd.

Calgary, Alberta, Canada

Aging in British Columbia

© 1998 Herbert C. Northcott and P. Jane Milliken

Canadian Cataloguing in Publication Data

Northcott, Herbert C., 1947-
Aging in British Columbia

Includes bibliographical references.
ISBN 1-55059-139-8

1. Aging—Social aspects—British Columbia.   2. Aged—British Columbia—Social conditions.   I. Milliken, Patricia Jane, 1947-   II. Title.
HQ1064.C2N672   1998   362.6'09711   C98-910101-0

Detselig Enterprises Ltd.
210-1220 Kensington Rd. N.W.
Calgary, Alberta T2N 3P5

Detselig Enterprises Ltd. appreciates the financial support for our 1998 publishing program, provided by Canadian Heritage and the Alberta Foundation for the Arts, a beneficiary of the Lottery Fund of the Government of Alberta.

Printed in Canada

ISBN 1-55059-139-8

SAN 115-0324

Cover design by Dean Macdonald.

Acknowledgments

We are most appreciative of our publisher's interest in this project and patience in waiting for a long-overdue manuscript. We also express appreciation to Charlene Marshall, who typed most of the many tables, Dave Odynak, who formatted the figures, Kerri Calvert, who provided library assistance, and Chuck Humphrey at the University of Alberta's Data Library, who provided access to health survey data files and to the 1996 "electronic" census data. Research assistance was provided by Kwame Boadu, Beth Chiasson, Brandy Green and Delaine Jodoin. Delaine Jodoin, Wendy Maurier and Michael Prince provided helpful suggestions.

Contents

1 Introduction   7

2 Population Aging in British Columbia   11

3 Fertility, Mortality and Migration in British Columbia . . .   27

4 The Demographic Characteristics of Seniors
  in British Columbia   49

5 The Health of Seniors in British Columbia   57

6 Public Policy and Programs for Seniors
  in British Columbia   71

7 Emerging Issues in Public Policy for Seniors
  in British Columbia   89

8 Seniors in British Columbia: Burden or Benefit? 115

References 125

Chapter One
Introduction

British Columbia is known as a province that attracts seniors. Many Canadians look forward to their retirement and many, especially those that live in the prairie provinces, consider following previous retirees to Canada's westernmost province. British Columbia has a lot to offer, in particular, an escape from long harsh winters. The mild climate, short winters and beautiful scenery beckon retirees and many heed the call. (For a discussion of the geographic mobility of seniors in Canada, see Northcott, 1988.)

It is a common perception that there are a lot of seniors living in British Columbia. This perception derives from the following logic. If seniors are moving from other provinces to British Columbia then there must be more seniors in that province than in other provinces. Furthermore, there appears to be evidence to support the perception of a substantial number of seniors in British Columbia. Places such as Victoria and the Okanagan are known to have a large proportion of senior residents.

While many seniors look forward to the benefits of retirement in British Columbia, non-seniors in British Columbia may be ambivalent or even worried about the influx of seniors. Another common perception among Canadians is that the population aging trend constitutes a challenge, problem or even a crisis (Northcott, 1997 and 1994). In other words, given the tendency to perceive seniors as "burdensome," the trend toward a relatively high concentration of seniors is often judged in negative terms.

The purpose of this book is to examine two perceptions: first, British Columbia is attracting a relatively high concentration of seniors, and second, this concentration of seniors is burdensome rather than beneficial. The first perception – that British Columbia has a high concentration of seniors relative to other Canadian provinces – is easily dealt with by reviewing current census data. A thorough examination of past, present and future trends in the concentration of seniors and the determinants of those trends produces an extensive array of statistics, tables and graphs. Some readers may prefer to avoid the statistics in chapters 2 through 5 and skip ahead to the policy discussions in chapters 6 to 8. Nevertheless, just to whet the reader's appetite for what follows, the statistical data show that common perceptions are often in error. In fact, it is a myth that British Columbia has the highest concentration of seniors among Canadian provinces. In 1996, British Columbia had only the fifth highest provincial concentration of seniors. Furthermore, from 1991 to 1996, British Columbia and Prince Edward Island were the only provinces in Canada to experience a <u>decline</u> in the seniors percentage of the population.

The second perception – that British Columbia's proclivity for attracting seniors is burdensome rather than beneficial – is not as easily dealt with. With any social change, there are "winners" and "losers." In other words, as seniors become more predominant in the population, there will be some who benefit more than others from this socio-demographic trend. Similarly, there will be some for whom this trend will be more costly. It follows that an assessment of benefit or burden depends in part on one's point of view.

Let us explore an extreme scenario. Suppose all Canadians who reach retirement age move to British Columbia. What consequences would this have for British Columbia, for each of the other provinces and for Canada as a whole?

Let's consider the implications first for old age income security and health care. Federal income support programs for seniors are the same regardless of province of residence and so the concentration of Canadian seniors in the province of British Columbia would have a negligible effect for the federal government. However, the provinces themselves may also provide various economic benefits to resident seniors. As seniors move to British Columbia, these benefit programs would become less costly for the sending provinces and indeed, would cost nothing if all of a province's seniors left for British Columbia. At the same time, these benefit programs would become more costly for British Columbia. Furthermore, given that health care is primarily a provincial responsibility, health care costs would tend to rise in British Columbia and fall in the other provinces. As British Columbia increasingly finds itself providing for the health care and other needs of Canada's seniors, one would expect British Columbia to begin to feel that it is increasingly shouldering an unfair burden. With the development of this perception, ageism might become rampant in the province. Furthermore, political strategies in the province might increasingly cut back seniors' programs and/or demand that the other provinces provide assistance or compensation to British Columbia.

Remember that this is an extreme and entirely implausible scenario. More realistically, one might ask to what extent the migration of seniors into British Columbia is disproportionate and to what extent the migration of seniors into British Columbia produces an unfair burden on that province.

Now, the above has been phrased entirely in the negative, as if all seniors individually and collectively are nothing more than a burden on the taxpayer, on the health care system and on social benefit programs. The truth is quite the opposite. Most individual seniors most of the time are reasonably healthy, happy and living independently (Northcott, 1997: 65). Many seniors pay taxes and/or make a variety of other contributions that reduce the burden of caring for needy Canadians, both young and old. Furthermore, seniors as a group bring certain benefits that help to offset any burden that they might bring. Indeed, let's return to the extreme scenario described above. If all of Canada's seniors moved to British Columbia, then all federal old age transfer payments to individual seniors would tend to end up in the British Columbia economy. Furthermore, both the Canada Pension Plan payments and all private pensions paid to seniors would also tend to be spent in the province of British Columbia. Many seniors are financially well off and seniors moving to British Columbia would tend to bring their Registered Retirement Savings Plans (RRSPs) and other life savings with them. Banking and other financial institutions would benefit from a large concentration of senior residents. The influx of seniors would also benefit the housing industry, as well as the travel and tourism industry. Furthermore, seniors make very little demand on educational institutions or on police services, saving the taxpayer expenses in these areas.

Once again, this is an extreme and entirely implausible scenario. Previously, this extreme scenario led us to ask to what extent the migration of seniors into British Columbia is disproportionate and to what extent the migration of seniors into British Columbia produces an unfair burden on that province. However, one might also ask to what extent the disproportionate migration of seniors into British Columbia produces windfall benefits for that province. It is the purpose of this monograph to examine population aging in British Columbia and to examine the degree to which seniors constitute a burden and/or benefit for that province.

Before launching into an examination of the "concentration" of seniors in British Columbia, it might help to clarify terminology. The concentration of seniors refers to the number of seniors out of every 100 persons of all ages in the population, or in other words, the *percentage* of the population that is seniors. For example, if a population has 10 seniors per 100 population, then seniors make up 10% of the population. Alternatively, concentration may be expressed in terms of the *proportion* of seniors in the population. In the above example, seniors make up one-tenth of the population. Concentration may also be assessed in terms of absolute numbers. For example, in a city of one million persons, there might be 100 000 seniors. Throughout this book, the concentration of seniors will be measured using the seniors percentage of the population, occasionally supplemented with absolute numbers.

Note that high concentrations do not necessarily imply large absolute numbers. A high concentration of seniors, say 25% of a local population, does not indicate a lot of seniors if the population is a village of 100 persons. Alternatively, a relatively low percentage of seniors in the population of a large city will account for a large number of seniors.

There are significant regional differences in Canada and these merit special attention from time to time (for comments on the development of local population studies in Britain, see Champion, 1993). Indeed, it can be argued that the maturation of the Canadian academic enterprise will be accompanied by the development of strong regional studies programs. By examining population aging in British Columbia, this project contributes to the development of regional studies in Canada. This is the second monograph in a series focusing on population aging in Canada's provinces. (The first study in this series was *Aging in Alberta*. See Northcott, 1997 and 1992.)

This examination of aging in British Columbia unfolds as follows. The following chapter shows the past, present and future percentages of seniors for British Columbia, including comparisons with other Canadian provinces. In addition, the seniors percentages and the seniors sex ratios in British Columbia's regional districts and selected urban areas are shown. While the term "sex ratio" might seem titillating, it is just another statistic. The sex ratio indicates the number of older men in comparison to the number of older women.

The changes in population age composition examined in chapter two are a function of trends in fertility, mortality and migration. These trends are examined in chapter three. Chapter four reports on additional aspects of the demography of population aging in British Columbia including the marital status, living arrangements and socio-economic status of seniors. Also included in chapter four is an examination of the so-called dependency ratio statistics. The dependency ratio indicates the number of seniors in comparison to the number of adults who are not seniors.

Chapters two through four, then, address the question: What are the trends in the concentration of seniors in British Columbia and why? The remaining chapters turn to the question of senior burden. Because seniors tend to be perceived as a burden on the health care system, chapter five reports the health status of seniors in British Columbia in comparison to Canadian seniors generally. In order to further address the issue of "burden," chapter six reviews the various programs that are supported by taxpayers for the benefit of seniors. Furthermore, because the perception of senior burden is widespread, chapter seven goes on to examine the extent to which trends in public policy are driven by allegations and perceptions of the increasing burden of an aging population. Finally, chapter eight critically examines the concept of senior burden and explores the various ways in which seniors can be a benefit as well as a burden.

Chapter Two
Population Aging in British Columbia

This chapter examines the aging trend in British Columbia by reporting past, present and projected concentrations of seniors in British Columbia. The concentration of seniors is measured by the seniors percentage of the population. This chapter also examines the concentration and distribution of seniors in British Columbia's census divisions (known in British Columbia as regional districts) and in the province's cities and towns.

Map 2.1: North America showing location of British Columbia

Map 2.2

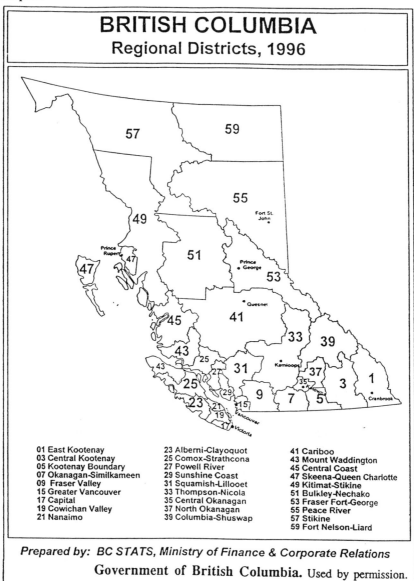

BRITISH COLUMBIA
Regional Districts, 1996

01 East Kootenay	23 Alberni-Clayoquot	41 Cariboo
03 Central Kootenay	25 Comox-Strathcona	43 Mount Waddington
05 Kootenay Boundary	27 Powell River	45 Central Coast
07 Okanagan-Similkameen	29 Sunshine Coast	47 Skeena-Queen Charlotte
09 Fraser Valley	31 Squamish-Lillooet	49 Kitimat-Stikine
15 Greater Vancouver	33 Thompson-Nicola	51 Bulkley-Nechako
17 Capital	35 Central Okanagan	53 Fraser Fort-George
19 Cowichan Valley	37 North Okanagan	55 Peace River
21 Nanaimo	39 Columbia-Shuswap	57 Stikine
		59 Fort Nelson-Liard

Prepared by: BC STATS, *Ministry of Finance & Corporate Relations*

Government of British Columbia. Used by permission.

A few historical and geographical notes are in order. British Columbia entered the newly formed Canadian confederation as a province on the 20th of July, 1871 (Granatstein, et al., 1990:26). British Columbia is Canada's most western province, with the Pacific Ocean defining its western boundary. To the south is the United States, with the Alaskan panhandle to the northwest. The Yukon and Northwest Territories lie to the north, while the province of Alberta defines the eastern boundary.

Map 2.3: Census Metropolitan Areas and Census Agglomerations in B.C., 1996

Source: Adapted from Statistics Canada. *1996 Census, A National Overview: Population and Dwelling Counts*. Catalogue number 93-357, Map showing Census Metropolitan Areas and Census Agglomerations, 1996. Used by permission.

The population of British Columbia in 1871 totalled 36 247 persons (Dominion Bureau of Statistics, 1936: 67-68). By 1996, the province's population had risen over 100 times to 3 724 500 (Statistics Canada, 1997a). Vancouver had become the third largest city in Canada with a census metropolitan area population of 1 831 665 in 1996. In other words, half of the population of the province of British Columbia in 1996 lived in Vancouver. The capital of the province is

Victoria, located on Vancouver Island, with a 1996 census metropolitan area population of 304 285 persons (Statistics Canada, 1997a).

In order to place British Columbia in national context, Table 2.1 shows the seniors percentage of the population for Canadian provinces and territories from 1881 to 1996. During this period of time, the seniors percentage of the population tended to increase for Canada as a whole and for each of the provinces. In other words, the population of Canada and the populations of each of the provinces have been "aging" and this population aging trend has been on-going for over a century. The primary causes of this population aging trend are declining fertility and increasing life expectancy, both of which are typical of industrializing countries. In addition, migration has also influenced the population aging trend.

Table 2.1 shows that the age structures and trends in the Northwest Territories and Yukon Territory through-out the 20th century have been substantially different from the age structures and trends in the provinces. While the data for the territories are shown in relevant tables, the following discussion focuses on the provinces and, in particular, the province of British Columbia.

In 1881, 1901 and 1921 the eastern provinces including Ontario, Quebec and the Maritime provinces had higher percentages of their populations which were seniors than did the western provinces. For example, in 1881 the population of British Columbia was 2.4% seniors in comparison to Nova Scotia, which had 5.1% seniors. By 1921, the population of British Columbia was 3.5 % seniors in comparison to Nova Scotia, which had seen its seniors increase to 7.3% of the population. These decades were a time of heavy migration from Europe to the prairie provinces and British Columbia. Given that migrants tended to be young adults, the resulting percentage of seniors in the population tended to be low in the western provinces during this period of time.

By 1941, the four western provinces had begun to catch up to the eastern provinces in terms of the seniors percentage of the population. Indeed, British Columbia at 8.3% seniors in 1941 surpassed Nova Scotia at 8.1% seniors. Among the provinces in both 1941 and 1961, British Columbia was second only to Prince Edward Island in terms of the seniors percentage of the population.

Following the Second World War, the Canadian population continued to age as life expectancy increased and as fertility decreased (although there was an upturn in fertility rates from 1946 to the early 1960s, which produced the "baby boom"). Furthermore, in the decades following the Second World War, Saskatchewan and Manitoba "aged" considerably as young people left the farms, villages and towns for jobs in the cities, often in other provinces. The post-war oil boom in Alberta attracted many such interprovincial migrants, especially during the 1970s. The exodus of young people from Saskatchewan and Manitoba meant that seniors who remained behind constituted a rising and relatively high percentage of the remaining population. In contrast, the influx of young people into Alberta helped that province maintain the lowest seniors percentage of all Canadian provinces. The migration of young adults to British Columbia also offset British Columbia's aging trend. In 1981, 1986 and 1991, the province of British Columbia had the fourth highest percent seniors, behind Saskatchewan,

Manitoba and Prince Edward Island. In 1996, British Columbia fell to fifth place as Nova Scotia once again joined the list of provinces with a higher percentage of seniors than British Columbia. Nevertheless, by 1996, 12.8% of British Columbia's population was seniors, as opposed to 2.4% in 1881.

Table 2.1: The Percentage of Seniors in the Canadian Population by Province and Census Year, 1881-1996

Province	Percentage 65 Years of Age and Older								
	1881	1901	1921	1941	1961	1981	1986	1991	1996
British Columbia	2.4	2.5	3.5	8.3	10.2	10.9	12.1	12.9	12.8
Alberta	na	1.8	2.3	5.2	7.0	7.3	8.1	9.1	9.9
Saskatchewan	na	2.5	2.3	5.2	9.2	12.0	12.7	14.1	14.7
Manitoba	1.6	2.4	3.1	6.3	9.0	11.9	12.6	13.4	13.7
Ontario	3.9	5.5	5.9	8.0	8.1	10.1	10.9	11.7	12.4
Quebec	4.3	4.8	4.6	5.3	5.8	8.8	10.0	11.2	12.1
New Brunswick	4.4	5.8	6.2	7.1	7.8	10.1	11.1	12.2	12.6
Nova Scotia	5.1	6.7	7.3	8.1	8.6	10.9	11.9	12.6	13.1
Prince Edward Island	4.5	6.8	9.6	9.4	10.4	12.2	12.7	13.2	13.0
Newfoundland	na	na	na	na	5.9	7.7	8.8	9.7	10.8
Northwest Territories	1.8	3.5	2.1	2.9	2.6	2.9	2.8	2.8	3.0
Yukon Territory	na	0.4	5.9	11.3	3.2	3.2	3.7	4.0	4.4
CANADA	4.1	5.1	4.8	6.7	7.6	9.7	10.7	11.6	12.2

Sources: Adapted from Statistics Canada. 1991 Census of Canada. Catalogue Number 93-310, Table 1 (for 1921-1991); Dominion Bureau of Statistics. Seventh Census of Canada, 1931, Volume 1, Pages 385-399 (for 1881-1931); Statistics Canada. *The Daily*, 29 July 1997 (for 1996).
na = not applicable

Figure 2.1 shows the age and sex composition of the population of British Columbia in 1901 and 1996. As is evident from these "population pyramids," the composition of the population of the province has changed substantially during the 20th century. In 1901, there were almost two males in British Columbia for every one female. This "sex ratio" was most discrepant for working age males, reflecting several decades of heavy in-migration by young adult males. In contrast, by 1996, there were slightly more females than males in the population of British Columbia (50.6% versus 49.4%). Furthermore, while in 1901 there were more males than females at every age (except over age 85), in 1996, females outnumbered males at ages 20-44 and ages 65 and older. This dramatic change in the overall sex ratio and in the age-specific sex ratios reflects more gender-balanced in-migration patterns (Johnston, 1996:181-184) and the greater improvement of female life expectancy in comparison to male life expectancy. As the difference between male and female life expectancy in-

Figure 2.1: Age and Sex Composition of British Columbia, 1901 and 1996

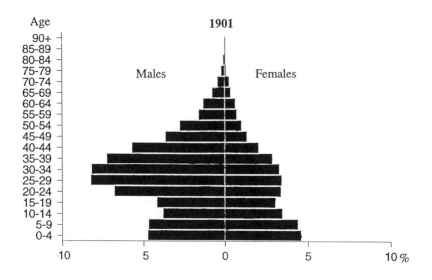

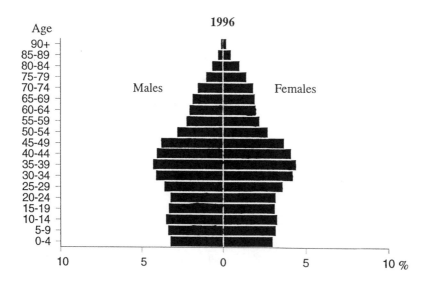

Sources: Adapted from Statistics Canada, 1998. The Nation Series, Edition 1 (Catalogue Number 9350020XCB96001). 1996 Census of Canada (CD-ROM). Ottawa: Ministry of Industry. Adapted from Dominion Bureau of Statistics. Seventh Census of Canada, 1931. Volume I, pages 392-393.

creased over the 20th century, the sex ratios for seniors increasingly showed a "shortage" of older men.

Finally, in 1996, in comparison to 1901, there were proportionately fewer young people under 15 years of age in British Columbia and proportionately more old people 65 years of age and over. This pattern is primarily a consequence of declining fertility resulting in relatively fewer children (and therefore relatively more older people) and increasing life expectancy resulting in relatively more seniors. As noted above, migration patterns tended to slow the population aging trend.

Figure 2.2 shows the trends from 1881 to 1996 in the percentages of the population of British Columbia for youth aged 0 to 14 and seniors aged 65 and older. The youth percentage declined from 1881 to 1911, rose briefly following the First World War, and then continued to decline through the 1920s and the depression years of the 1930s. The baby boom following the Second World War reversed this trend and the youth percentage rose in 1951 and again in 1961. Since then, a pattern of decline in the youth percentage of the population has again been evident.

Declining fertility and downward trends in the youth percentage of the population imply increases in the percentages of the older segments of the population. However, from 1881 to 1911, the seniors percentage of the population of British Columbia remained fairly level, partly as a result of the in-migration of young adults. The seniors percentage then increased from 1911 to 1951. In 1961 and 1971, the seniors percentage declined as a result of the baby boom. In 1981 and 1991, the aging trend is once again evident, although the seniors percentage dropped slightly from 12.9% in 1991 to 12.8% in 1996, largely because of exceptionally high in-migration during the 1991-1996 period (Statistics Canada, 1997b:3; Statistics Canada, 1997c:2).

Figure 2.2: Percentage of Seniors and Youth in the Population of British Columbia, 1881-1996

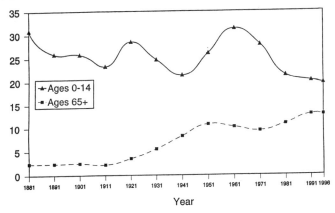

Sources: Adapted from – for 1996: StatsCan. *The Daily*, 29 July 1997; for 1941-1991: StatsCan. 1991 Census of Canada. Catalogue Number 93-310, Table 1; for 1881-1931: Dominion Bureau of Stats. 7th Census of Canada, 1931. Volume 1, Pages 398-399.

Figure 2.3 shows the age and sex composition and the age-specific sex ratios for seniors in British Columbia for 1911, 1931, 1951, 1971 and 1991. The aging trend is evident in the increasing percentages of seniors in each age category. The only break in this pattern of population aging is a temporary decrease in the percentages of the younger elderly (in the 1971 data) as a result of the baby boom depressing the percentage share of seniors.

The 1991 and the 1971 data show a preponderance of females in the seniors population. Indeed, the age-specific sex ratios (the number of males of a specific age per 100 females of the same age) show that there are currently substantially more women than men for all ages over 65. Furthermore, this discrepancy increases with increasing age. This pattern is the result of differences in female and male life expectancy. Females currently live substantially longer, on average, than do males.

This discrepancy in female and male life expectancy has not always been, nor will it necessarily continue in the future. In fact, there is evidence that the sex differential in life expectancy has begun to converge (Wilkins, 1996; Millar, 1995) as females approach the biological upper age limit for the human species and as men begin to "catch up." Nevertheless, a substantial differential currently exists and females will predominate among seniors for decades to come.

Female life expectancy has not always been so favorable. The data for 1911, for example, show that men outnumbered women at all ages over 65 in British Columbia. Furthermore, the data for 1931 and 1951 show that men outnumbered women at all ages from 65 to 84. As noted earlier, this pattern is primarily a function of heavy in-migration to British Columbia of young adult males for several decades before and after the turn of the century. Nevertheless, this pattern also reflects the more equal patterns of male and female life expectancy at that time in history. At that time, maternal mortality was still relatively high, and of course, the mortal risks of child-bearing were borne by women alone. Nevertheless, the 1911, 1931 and 1951 data show that the sex ratio decreased with increasing age, indicating that older women who survived their reproductive years have long enjoyed a greater life expectancy than older men of the same age.

In summary, Figure 2.3 illustrates the population aging trend in British Columbia. This figure also shows that the sex ratio has shifted from a preponderance of males among seniors at the beginning of the 20th century to a preponderance of females at the end of the century. Figure 2.3 further indicates that the sex ratio tends to decline with increasing age, meaning that women tend to increasingly outnumber men at the oldest ages due to their longer life expectancy.

The aging trend will continue well into the 21st century. Statistics Canada (1994) projections to 2016 indicate that British Columbia's seniors percentage will rise from 12.9% in 1991 to around 16% by 2016, under "medium growth" projection assumptions.

Table 2.2 shows the medium growth projection data for all of the provinces. In this projection, British Columbia is expected to have a seniors percentage in

Figure 2.3: Age and Sex Composition of the Seniors Population in B.C., 1911-1991

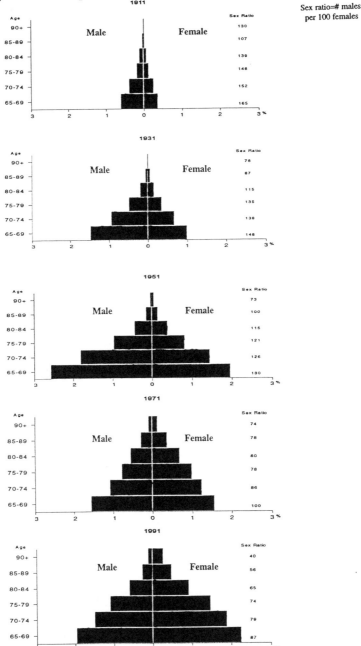

Sources: Adapted from Dominion Bureau of Statistics, 1931 Census, Vol. I, pp. 392-393. StatsCan., 1971 Census of Canada, Table 7, Cat. 92-715. StatsCan., 1991 Census of Canada, Table 4, Cat. 93-310.

2016 that will be somewhat lower than most of the other provinces. The Atlantic provinces, Saskatchewan and Quebec are expected to have relatively high seniors percentages. The so-called "have" provinces of British Columbia, Ontario and Alberta, which tend to have stronger economies and higher rates of growth, are expected to have somewhat lower seniors percentages. These three provinces attract migrants both from within Canada and internationally. In-migration of working age migrants tends to dampen the aging trend while the out-migration of working age persons tends to heighten the aging trend.

Table 2.2: The Projected Percentage of Seniors in the Canadian Population by Province, 1996 to 2016.

Province	Percentage 65 Years of Age and Older (Projected)				
	1996	2001	2006	2011	2016
British Columbia	13.1	13.3	13.5	14.4	16.3
Alberta	9.8	10.5	11.1	12.2	14.1
Saskatchewan	14.8	15.4	15.1	15.6	17.2
Manitoba	13.6	13.7	13.8	14.5	16.2
Ontario	12.3	12.5	12.8	13.5	15.1
Quebec	12.1	12.8	13.5	15.0	17.0
New Brunswick	12.7	13.2	14.0	15.6	18.5
Nova Scotia	13.1	13.6	14.3	15.8	18.5
Prince Edward Island	13.3	13.4	14.0	15.2	17.6
Newfoundland	10.4	11.3	12.6	14.8	18.4
Northwest Territories	3.6	4.5	5.3	6.2	7.9
Yukon Territory	4.6	5.6	6.9	8.9	10.5
CANADA	12.2	12.6	13.1	14.1	15.9

Source: Adapted from StatsCan, 1994. Population Projection for Canada, Provinces and Territories 1993-2016. Ottawa: Ministry of Industry, Science and Technology. Table A3, Projection Number 2: Medium Growth Projection. (Assumptions: Continuation of current trends including constant fertility of 1.7 births per woman, constant immigration of 250 000, and life expectancy rising to 78.5 years for males and 84.0 years for females by 2016 [see page 65])

In British Columbia, there are substantial variations from one part of the province to another in the concentration of seniors. Table 2.3 reports the concentration of seniors and the seniors sex ratios in 1996 in British Columbia's census divisions (known in British Columbia as regional districts). The following table, Table 2.4, reports the concentration of seniors and the seniors sex ratios for 1996 in British Columbia's two census metropolitan areas – Vancouver and Victoria – and for 1991 in British Columbia's "census agglomerations," that is, in places with an urbanized core of between 10 000 and 100 000 people.

Table 2.3: The Percentage of Seniors in the Population and the Seniors Sex Ratio for Census Divisions in B.C., 1996

Census Division	65+ Years of Age		
	Number	% of Population	Sex Ratio[1]
01. East Kootenay Regional District	6320	11.2	84
03. Central Kootenay Regional District	8570	14.8	86
05. Kootenay Boundary Regional District	5570	16.9	81
07. Okanagan-Similkameen Regional District	18 045	23.8	85
09. Fraser Valley Regional District	30 420	13.7	81
15. Greater Vancouver Regional District	216 425	11.8	73
17. Capital Regional District	57 470	18.1	69
19. Cowichan Valley Regional District	10 690	15.1	88
21. Nanaimo Regional District	20 920	17.2	85
23. Alberni-Clayaquot Regional District	3700	11.7	83
25. Comox-Strathcona Regional District	10 755	11.0	88
27. Powell River Regional District	2935	14.7	85
29. Sunshine Coast Regional District	4295	17.2	88
31. Squamish-Lillooet Regional District	1745	5.9	94
33. Thompson-Nicola Regional District	12 850	10.8	88
35. Central Okanagan Regional District	23 355	17.1	80
37. North Okanagan Regional District	11 555	16.1	83
39. Columbia-Shuswap Regional District	7150	14.9	92
41. Cariboo Regional District	5655	8.5	102
43. Mount Waddington Regional District	595	4.1	109
45. Central Coast Regional District	255	6.5	100
47. Skeena-Queen Charlotte Regional District	1495	6.0	87
49. Kitimat-Stikine Regional District	2565	5.9	102
51. Bulkley-Nechako Regional District	2910	7.0	104
53. Fraser-Fort George Regional District	5645	5.7	93
55. Peace River Regional District	3740	6.6	94
57. Stikine Regional District	70	5.0	100
59. Fort Nelson-Liard Regional District	130	2.2	100
BRITISH COLUMBIA	475 840	12.8	78

[1]Number of males aged 65+ per 100 females aged 65+
Source: Adapted from StatsCan., 1997. The Nation Series, Edition 1 (StatsCan. Cat. # 9350020XCB96001). 1996 Census of Canada (CD-ROM). Ottawa: Minister of Industry.

Table 2.4: % Seniors in the Population of Large Urban Centres (Census Metro-politan Areas & Census Agglomerations) in B.C. & Seniors Sex Ratio, 1991.

Urban Centres	65+ Years of Age		
	Number	% of Population	Sex Ratio[1]
Census Metropolitan Areas[2]			
Vancouver 1991	195 430	12.2	70
Vancouver 1996[3]	216 425	11.8	73
Victoria 1991	53 475	18.6	68
Victoria 1996	54 395	17.9	68
Census Agglomerations[4]			
Campbell River	2605	8.4	79
Chilliwack	9240	15.3	81
Courtenay	6015	13.5	85
Cranbrook	1770	10.8	71
Dawson Creek	990	9.0	77
Duncan	4205	15.4	77
Fort St. John	760	5.4	83
Kamloops	6605	9.7	80
Kelowna	19 690	17.6	83
Kitimat	420	3.7	100
Matsqui	15 455	13.6	81
Nanaimo	10 550	14.3	80
Penticton	10 380	23.0	82
Port Alberni	3010	11.3	82
Powell River	2490	13.5	80
Prince George	3550	5.1	87
Prince Rupert	1130	6.1	82
Quesnel	1770	7.6	99
Terrace	1005	5.3	91
Vernon	7655	15.9	81
Williams Lake	2755	7.9	100

[1]Number of males aged 65+ per 100 females aged 65+.
[2]A census agglomeration (CA) is a large urban area including economically and socially integrated adjacent urban and rural areas. The urban core of a CA has a population of at least 10 000. A census metropolitan area (CMA) on the other hand has an urban core of at least 100 000.
[3]1996 data were available for CMAs but not CAs
Source: Adapted from StatsCan. 1991 Census of Canada. Profile of Census Metro-politan Areas and Census Agglomerations. Cat. #93-337. Table 1. For source of 1996 CMA data, see Table 2.5 following.

Table 2.3 reports the distribution and concentration of seniors as well as the seniors sex ratio for the census divisions (CDs) in British Columbia. In very general terms, the distribution of seniors follows the distribution of the population. That is, the largest number of seniors (216 425 in 1996; 45% of all seniors in B.C.) reside in the Greater Vancouver census division. The second largest number of seniors (57 470 in 1996; 12% of all seniors) is found in the Capital census division, which includes the city of Victoria. Large numbers of seniors (10 000 or more seniors per census division in 1996) also reside in the census divisions of Fraser Valley, Central Okanagan, Nanaimo, Okanagan-Similkameen, Thompson-Nicola (which includes the city of Kamloops), North Okanagan, Comox-Strathcona and Cowichan Valley. A total of 412 000 seniors – 87% of all seniors in British Columbia – resided in these census divisions in 1996.

The concentration of seniors, that is, the seniors percentage of the population in a census division, varies substantially, from a low of 2.2% in the far north-east corner of the province (Fort Nelson-Liard) to a high of 23.8% in the south central Okanagan-Similkameen census division. The census divisions in the entire northern three-quarters of the province (CDs 41-59) have single-digit concentrations of seniors (2.2% to 8.5%). Except for CD 31, the southern CDs (1-39) have double-digit concentrations of seniors. The highest seniors percentages are found in the south central CDs (Central Kootenay with 14.8% seniors in 1996, Kootenay Boundary 16.9%, Okanagan-Similkameen 23.8%, Central Okanagan 17.1% and North Okanagan 16.1%), on Vancouver Island (Capital CD 18.1%, Cowichan Valley 15.1% and Nanaimo 17.2%) and in the Sunshine Coast 17.2%, Powell River 14.7% and Columbia-Shuswap 14.9% CDs.

The seniors sex ratios also vary substantially from one CD to another, ranging, in 1996, from a low of 69 in the Capital CD and 73 in the Greater Vancouver CD to a high of 109 in the Mount Waddington CD. The seniors sex ratio records the number of men 65 years of age and older per every 100 women 65 years of age and older. The sex ratio generally is below 100, indicating a preponderance of older women and a relative shortage of older men. The seniors sex ratio tends to be substantially lower than 100 in the more southerly census divisions.

In summary, most of British Columbia's seniors are found in the lower mainland, on Vancouver Island and in the Okanagan. In these areas, seniors make up substantial percentages of the population. In addition, seniors in these areas are disproportionately female. Away from these southerly areas of the province, seniors make up relatively small percentages of the population and there tend to be more equal numbers of older women and older men.

Table 2.4 reports the distribution and concentration of seniors as well as the seniors sex ratios for the two census metropolitan areas (CMAs) in 1991 and 1996 and the 21 census agglomerations (CAs) in British Columbia in 1991. (The 1996 census data for the CAs were not available at the time of writing.) The Victoria CMA in 1996 had a population of 54 395 seniors, making up 17.9% of the population of Victoria. The majority (60%) of these seniors were women. The Vancouver CMA in 1996 had a population of 216 425 seniors, making up

11.8% of the population of Vancouver. Again, the majority (58%) of these seniors were women.

The most populous census agglomerations in British Columbia in terms of seniors are in the Okanagan, the Fraser Valley and on Vancouver Island. These CAs include Kelowna (19 690 seniors in 1991, making up 17.6% of the population), Penticton (10 380 seniors and 23.0% of the population) and Vernon (7655 seniors and 15.9% of the population), Matsqui – renamed Abbotsford in the 1996 census – (15 455 seniors, 13.6%), Chilliwack (9240 seniors, 15.3%), Nanaimo (10 550 seniors, 14.3%) and Courtenay (6015 seniors, 13.5%). Kamloops had 6605 seniors, making up 9.7% of its population.

In total, in 1991 the CMAs of Vancouver and Victoria and the CAs of Kelowna, Penticton, Vernon, Matsqui, Chilliwack, Nanaimo, Courtenay and Kamloops had a combined population of 334 500 seniors. This total represented 79.3% of all seniors in British Columbia. Another 26 500 seniors (6.3%) lived in the remaining 13 CAs in British Columbia. This left 61 000 seniors (14.5%) living in smaller centres or in the rural areas of the province.

Table 2.4 also reports the seniors sex ratios for the CMAs and CAs in British Columbia. The seniors sex ratios in Victoria and Vancouver in 1996 were 68 and 73 respectively indicating a predominance of older women. The seniors sex ratios in the CAs in 1991 ranged from 71 in Cranbrook to 99 in Quesnel and 100 in Kitimat and Williams Lake. Most of the CAs had sex ratios close to 80, again indicating a predominance of older women.

A comparison of the data (not shown) for the cities proper with the CAs and CMAs (which include adjacent urban and rural areas) indicates that the central urban cores of the CAs and CMAs tend to have even higher percentages of seniors and a greater predominance of older women. The most extreme example in 1991 was Duncan. The city of Duncan had 1200 seniors making up 27.8% of the population. In comparison, the CA of Duncan had 4200 seniors making up 15.4% of the population. Further, the city of Duncan had a seniors sex ratio of 57, in comparison to the CA of Duncan, which had a seniors sex ratio of 77. Similarly, the city of Victoria had 17 000 seniors, making up 23.9% of the population, and a seniors sex ratio of 52. The CMA of Victoria had 53 500 seniors, making up 18.6% of the population, and a seniors sex ratio of 68. Finally, the city of Vernon had 5000 seniors for 21.3% of the population and a seniors sex ratio of 71. The CA of Vernon had 7655 seniors for 15.9% of the population and a sex ratio of 81. In short, the central urban cores tend to have a higher percentage of seniors and a greater preponderance of older women. The urban and rural fringes tend to have more non-seniors and a more equal seniors sex ratio.

Table 2.5 shows the seniors percentage of the population and the seniors sex ratio for all of the CMAs in Canada in 1996. Canada's 25 CMAs had a combined population of 2 069 795 seniors, totaling 59% of all seniors in the country. The seniors percentages were lowest in Calgary (8.7%), Edmonton (9.8%) and Oshawa (9.8%) and highest in Victoria (17.9%) and St. Catharines-Niagara (16.3%). The seniors sex ratios ranged from 60 in Quebec City to 77 in Sudbury, indicating that every CMA in Canada has a preponderance of older women among its senior population.

Table 2.5: Percentage of Seniors in the Population in Census Metropolitan Areas in Canada and Seniors Sex Ratio, 1996

Census Metropolitan Areas	65+ Years of Age		
	Number	% of Population	Sex Ratio[1]
Newfoundland			
St. John's	17 385	10.0	65
Nova Scotia			
Halifax	33 590	10.1	66
New Brunswick			
Saint John	15 865	12.6	66
Quebec			
Chicoutimi-Jonquière	17 270	10.8	68
Montreal	400 135	12.0	65
Quebec City	78 180	11.6	60
Sherbrooke	18 020	12.2	61
Trois-Rivières	18 370	13.1	62
Quebec-Ontario			
Ottawa-Hull	102 675	10.2	67
Ontario			
Hamilton	86 580	13.9	73
Kitchener	41 650	10.9	67
London	50 315	12.6	68
Oshawa	26 410	9.8	73
St. Catharines-Niagara	60 670	16.3	73
Sudbury	18 850	11.7	77
Thunder Bay	17 675	14.1	74
Toronto	467 580	11.0	72
Windsor	36 080	12.9	68
Manitoba			
Winnipeg	88 820	13.3	66
Saskatchewan			
Regina	22 775	11.8	68
Saskatoon	24 480	11.2	69
Alberta			
Calgary	71 480	8.7	73
Edmonton	84 140	9.8	74
British Columbia			
Vancouver	216 425	11.8	73
Victoria	54 395	17.9	68

[1]Number of males aged 65+ per 100 females aged 65+.
Source: www.statcan.ca, 1996 Census bin, Population by Selected Age Groups and Sex for Census Metropolitan Areas (100% Data). Accessed 5 November 1997.

The seniors percentage of the population of British Columbia has increased substantially from 2.4% in 1881 to 12.8% in 1996. In general terms, the distribution of seniors in 1996 follows the distribution of the population. That is, the largest numbers of seniors reside in the Greater Vancouver and Capital (Victoria) Regional Districts (census divisions). The most southerly census divisions in 1996 tend to have high seniors percentages, reaching 23.8% in the Okanagan-Similkameen CD. The most southerly census divisions in 1996 also tend to have more older women than older men. In contrast, the northern three-quarters of the province tends to have low seniors percentages and more equal numbers of older women and men.

The population aging trend in British Columbia has been a function of changing patterns of fertility, mortality and migration. The next chapter examines the trends in fertility, mortality and migration in the province of British Columbia.

Chapter Three
Fertility, Mortality and Migration in British Columbia

Population aging is a function of trends in fertility, mortality and migration. Fertility, mortality, and migration describe the ways in which people enter and exit a population. These patterns of entrances and exits determine both population size and population composition. For example, population age composition is a function of the entry of young people through birth, the exit of people of various ages through death, and the entry and exit of people of various ages through migration.

Population age composition is determined primarily by the combination of mortality and fertility. Decreasing mortality rates mean increasing life expectancy, or in other words, a greater percentage of persons surviving to older ages. Decreasing fertility rates mean that there are relatively fewer young people entering the population thereby allowing the seniors percentage to increase. On the other hand, high mortality (i.e., relatively few people living to old age) coupled with high fertility (i.e., relatively large numbers of babies being born) will result in a low percentage of seniors in the population. Finally, fertility and mortality trends may offset each other. For example, low mortality which contributes to population aging may be offset by high fertility which produces a more youthful population.

Migration also contributes to population age composition. The in-migration of seniors increases the seniors percentage while the in-migration of non-seniors has the opposite effect and reduces the seniors percentage. In other words, the in-migration of seniors and non-seniors tends to be counterbalancing. Similarly, the out-migration of seniors decreases the seniors percentage while the out-migration of non-seniors has the opposite effect and increases the seniors percentage in the remaining population. Nevertheless, the migration patterns of seniors and non-seniors are not necessarily counterbalancing. For example, population aging would tend to be most enhanced in places where there is in-migration of seniors and out-migration of non-seniors.

This chapter examines trends in fertility, mortality and migration in British Columbia and the impact of these trends on population aging in that province. Figure 3.1 shows trends in the standardized general fertility rate, which is the number of children born per 1000 women aged 15 to 49, standardized to the 1971 Canadian female population. Standardization holds age composition constant allowing for valid comparisons both over time and for different populations. Trends are shown for both Canada and British Columbia from 1921 to 1990.

From 1921 through 1952, fertility rates were lower in British Columbia than in Canada as a whole. This pattern helped British Columbia age faster than Canada as a whole during this time. From 1953 to 1990, fertility rates in British Columbia have been comparable to the Canadian average.

Fertility in British Columbia declined from 82 births per 1000 women aged 15 to 49 in 1921 to a low of 55 in the midst of the depression of the 1930s. Declining fertility contributed to population aging during that period of time. Fertility in British Columbia then trended upward peaking in 1959 at a rate of 123 births, a rate fully 50% higher than in 1921. This "baby boom" tended to reverse the population aging trend with the effect most notable from 1951 to 1971. From 1960 to 1976 the fertility rate in British Columbia declined, dropping to 54 births per 1000 women aged 15 to 49 in 1976. This fertility rate passed the previous low of 55 in 1935. Fertility has remained in the lower 50s from 1976 through 1990. Low fertility has once again contributed to population aging in British Columbia.

Figure 3.1: Standardized General Fertility Rates for British Columbia and Canada, 1921-1990

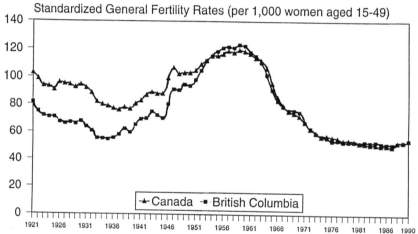

Source: StatsCan, 1993. Selected Birth and Fertility Statistics, Canada 1921-1990. Cat. #82-553, Table 2 (SFGR is the birth rate per 1000 women 15-49 years of age, standardized to the 1971 Canadian female population)

Figure 3.2 shows trends in male and female death rates, standardized to the 1991 Canadian population. Death rates for both British Columbia and Canada as a whole are shown for 1950 through 1990. Female death rates have been consistently lower than male death rates during the last half of the 20th century producing, as a result, a sex ratio in old age that favors females. That is, there are more older females than older males because females on average live longer than males. From 1950 through 1990, mortality rates were lower in British Columbia than in Canada as a whole. Figure 3.2 also shows that male and female death rates for both British Columbia and Canada as a whole have declined from 1950 to 1990. Declining death rates mean increasing life expectancy and contribute to the aging of the population.

Figure 3.2: Standardized Death Rates for British Columbia and Canada, 1950-1990

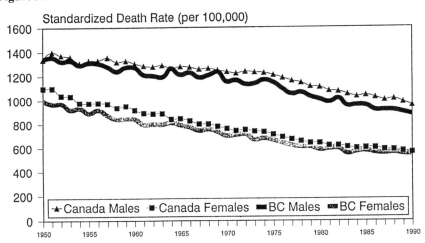

Source: StatsCan., 1994. Selected Mortality Statistics, Canada, 1921-1990. Cat. #82-548,
Table 3. (Standard population is Canada, 1991).

Besides fertility and mortality, population composition is influenced by
migration trends. Table 3.1 shows the place of birth for seniors and non-seniors
in Canada's provinces in 1991. Only 20% of the seniors residing in British
Columbia in 1991 were born in that province, meaning that 80% of seniors in
British Columbia in 1991 had moved into the province at some previous time in
their life. This 20% figure is by far the lowest of all the provinces. In contrast,
the next lowest figure is 42% for Alberta. That is, 42% of seniors residing in
Alberta in 1991 were born in that province. In Ontario, 50% of resident seniors
were born in that province while in Quebec and the Atlantic Provinces the figure
tends to be over 80% with a high of 97% in Newfoundland. A similar pattern is
evident for non-seniors. These figures mean that there has been relatively little
in-migration into the provinces east of Ontario and relatively high in-migration
into the provinces west of Quebec, especially into British Columbia, Alberta and
Ontario.

Table 3.1 also shows the percentages of resident populations in 1991 that were
born in other Canadian provinces or in other countries. While this table also
shows the data for the territories, the following discussion focuses on the
provinces. Population dynamics in the territories are quite different than in the
provinces. Accordingly, the territories warrant a separate in-depth study. The
percentages of the senior populations of the eastern provinces born in other
provinces or in other countries tend to be relatively low. On the other hand, a
relatively high percentage of both seniors and non-seniors in Ontario were born
in other countries. Furthermore, relatively high percentages of seniors and
non-seniors in Alberta and British Columbia were born in both other provinces
and in other countries. Indeed, British Columbia had the highest percent seniors
in 1991 born in other provinces (43%) and in other countries (37%). In short,

British Columbia has had a strong attraction for migrants from other Canadian provinces and from other countries. The impact of this migration on the population age structure of British Columbia depends on the age of the migrants at the time of their migration to the province. In-migration of seniors adds to the population aging trend while in-migration of non-seniors tends to counterbalance population aging.

Table 3.1: Province of Residence in 1991 by Age and Place of Birth

Province of Residence and Age Group in 1991	Born in Province of Current Residence	Born in Other Province	Canadian-born, but born Outside Canada	Immigrant, born in Other Country	Total	
	%	%	%	%	%	(n)
Newfoundland						
0-64	93.1	5.4	0.1	1.4	100.0	(512 065)
65+	96.5	1.3	0.0	2.2	100.0	(51 035)
Prince Edward Island						
0-64	79.3	17.7	0.3	2.7	100.0	(112 310)
65+	82.4	10.7	0.2	6.8	100.1	(15 670)
Nova Scotia						
0-64	79.8	16.0	0.3	3.9	100.0	(782 905)
65+	79.7	12.0	0.2	8.1	100.0	(106 340)
New Brunswick						
0-64	82.8	13.9	0.3	3.0	100.0	(633 590)
65+	82.6	10.9	0.2	6.3	100.0	(81 550)
Quebec						
0-64	88.0	3.6	0.2	8.2	100.0	(6 061 995)
65+	81.5	5.3	0.2	13.0	100.0	(704 340)
Ontario						
0-64	67.4	9.6	0.4	22.5	99.9	(8 756 820)
65+	50.1	13.3	0.4	36.2	100.0	(1 094 070)
Manitoba						
0-64	74.6	13.6	0.4	11.4	100.0	(938 730)
65+	62.8	13.8	0.3	23.1	100.0	(136 630)
Saskatchewan						
0-64	82.7	12.8	0.2	4.3	100.0	(844 305)
65+	71.6	11.2	0.5	16.7	100.0	(128 855)
Alberta						
0-64	59.1	26.8	0.4	13.8	100.1	(2 295 780)
65+	41.7	26.4	0.5	31.4	100.0	(209 320)

Table 3.1: Province of Residence in 1991 by Age and Place of Birth

Province of Residence and Age Group in 1991	Place of Birth				Total	
	Born in Province of Current Residence	Born in Other Province	Canadian-born, but born Outside Canada	Immigrant, born in Other Country		
	%	%	%	%	%	(n)
British Columbia						
0-64	52.8	26.3	0.4	20.5	100.0	(2 826 805
65+	20.2	42.7	0.4	36.7	100.0	(392 660)
Yukon Territory						
0-64	34.0	55.3	0.4	10.3	100.0	(26 535)
65+	22.3	54.9	0.0	22.8	100.0	(1030)
Northwest Territories						
0-64	56.8	38.1	0.2	4.8	99.9	(55 775)
65+	72.7	19.0	0.3	8.0	100.0	(1500)

Source: Adapted from StatsCan. *Immigration and citizenship.* Ottawa: Supply and Services Canada, 1992. 1991 Census of Canada. Cat. #93-316. Tables 3 & 4.

Table 3.2 examines the age of recent migrants. The 1991 census was the first census to ask residents, excluding persons living in institutions such as nursing homes, where they lived one year earlier. In other words, Table 3.2 shows the "one-year mobility status" of persons in Canada from 1990 to 1991. For Canada as a whole, some 82% of non-seniors and 94% of seniors had not moved in that year. On the other hand, 18% of non-seniors and 6% of seniors had changed their residence in the past year. Most of those who had changed their address moved within their province of residence. Relatively small percentages moved from one province to another or moved to Canada from another country. Indeed, for Canada as a whole, 4 in 1000 seniors changed their province of residence in 1990-1991 while another 3 in 1000 seniors came to Canada from another country.

Excluding the territories, Alberta and British Columbia had the highest rates of in-migration from other Canadian provinces for both seniors and non-seniors in 1990-1991. Eight in 1000 seniors in both Alberta and British Columbia had come from other Canadian provinces in the previous year. While this high rate of in-migration of seniors contributes to population aging, the higher rate of in-migration of non-seniors counterbalances the aging trend.

Table 3.2: One-Year Mobility Status, 1990-91, by Age and Province of Residence

Province of Residence and Age Group, 1991	Population 1+ Years of Age*	Non-movers	Total Movers	Intra-Provincial Movers	Inter-Provincial In-Migrants	Inter-national In-Migrants
	(n)	%	%	%	%	%
CANADA						
1-64	(23 530 805)	82.3	17.7	15.4	1.3	1.0
65+	(2 900 090)	94.2	5.8	5.1	0.4	0.3
Newfoundland						
1-64	(503 665)	87.9	12.1	9.8	2.0	0.2
65+	(50 805)	96.3	3.7	3.3	0.3	0.1
Prince Edward Island						
1-64	(109 610)	86.9	13.2	10.6	2.2	0.3
65+	(15 365)	95.7	4.3	3.7	0.6	0.1
Nova Scotia						
1-64	(766 610)	84.4	15.6	12.9	2.3	0.4
65+	(105 515)	95.9	4.1	3.5	0.5	0.1
New Brunswick						
1-64	(621 555)	86.5	13.5	11.2	2.0	0.3
65+	(80 885)	95.7	4.3	3.9	0.4	0.0
Quebec						
1-64	(5 979 470)	84.6	15.4	14.3	0.4	0.6
65+	(687 380)	94.5	5.5	5.2	0.1	0.2
Ontario						
1-64	(8 691 245)	83.1	16.9	14.9	0.8	1.2
65+	(1 092 785)	94.7	5.3	4.6	0.2	0.5
Manitoba						
1-64	(912 715)	82.6	17.4	14.9	1.8	0.7
65+	(135 460)	94.5	5.5	4.9	0.4	0.2
Saskatchewan						
1-64	(824 815)	83.2	16.8	14.4	2.0	0.4
65+	(128 315)	95.2	4.8	4.3	0.4	0.1
Alberta						
1-64	(2 246 335)	77.3	22.7	19.1	2.7	1.0
65+	(208 355)	93.4	6.6	5.4	0.8	0.4
British Columbia						
1-64	(2 795 280)	76.6	23.4	19.2	2.6	1.5
65+	(392 720)	91.5	8.5	7.2	0.8	0.5

Table 3.2: One-Year Mobility Status, 1990-91, by Age and Province of Residence

Province of Residence and Age Group, 1991	Population 1+ Years of Age*	Non-movers	Total Movers	Intra-Provincial Movers	Inter-Provincial In-Migrants	Inter-national In-Migrants
			Movers, 1990-91			
	(n)	%	%	%	%	%
Yukon Territory						
1-64	(24 685)	73.4	26.6	18.5	7.5	0.6
65+	(1025)	88.8	11.2	5.9	4.9	0.0
Northwest Territories						
1-64	(53 830)	71.8	28.2	21.5	6.3	0.3
65+	(1475)	88.1	11.9	10.5	1.4	0.0

Percentages may not add exactly to totals due to rounding.
*Persons under one year of age are excluded because they did not have a previous residence one year earlier.
Source: Adapted from StatsCan. Mobility and migration. Ottawa: Industry, Science and Technology, Canada, 1993. 1991 Census of Canada, Cat. #93-322, Table 1B. (20% sample. Excludes persons institutionalized in previous six or more months.)

With respect to international migration, British Columbia, Ontario and Alberta had the highest rates of in-migration from other countries for both seniors and non-seniors in 1990-1991. Five in 1000 seniors in both British Columbia and Ontario (and 4 in 1000 in Alberta) had come from other countries in the previous year. While this high rate of in-migration of seniors contributes to population aging, again the higher rate of in-migration of non-seniors counterbalances the aging trend.

The 1991 census also asked where people lived at the time of the previous census five years earlier. Table 3.3 shows the "five-year mobility status" of the population. For Canada as a whole over the five-year period from 1986 to 1991, some 50% of non-seniors and about 22% of seniors made at least one change of residence. As seen above, most changes of residence are relatively short distance intra-provincial moves. Nevertheless, 15 seniors per 1000 changed their province of residence in the 1986-1991 period, while 13 seniors per 1000 arrived in Canada from other countries during that period of time.

Of all Canadian provinces (and with the exception of the territories), British Columbia had the highest rates of mobility for both seniors and non-seniors during 1986-1991. British Columbia also had the highest rates of in-migration from other Canadian provinces for both seniors and non-seniors. In 1991, almost 4 in every 100 seniors residing in British Columbia had arrived in the province from other Canadian provinces in the previous five years. While this in-migration of seniors into British Columbia from other provinces tends to contribute to population aging, the in-migration of non-seniors counterbalances the aging trend (see also Bergob, 1995).

Table 3.3: Five-Year Mobility Status, 1986-91, by Age and Province of Residence in 1991

Province of Residence and Age Group, 1991	Population 5+ Years of Age*	Non-movers	Total Movers	Intra-Provincial Movers	Inter-Provincial In-Migrants	Inter-National In-Migrants
			Movers 1986-91			
	(n)	%	%	%	%	%
CANADA						
5-64	(22 027 780)	50.1	49.9	41.7	4.2	4.0
65+	(2 900 090)	77.8	22.2	19.5	1.5	1.3
Newfoundland						
5-64	(474 040)	69.8	30.2	25.4	4.3	0.6
65+	(50 805)	88.5	11.5	10.4	0.9	0.1
Prince Edward Island						
5-64	(102 120)	62.6	37.4	28.4	8.2	0.9
65+	(15 370)	84.7	15.3	12.0	2.6	0.7
Nova Scotia						
5-64	(718 335)	58.6	41.4	33.1	7.1	1.1
65+	(105 515)	85.0	15.0	12.6	2.0	0.4
New Brunswick						
5-64	(583 705)	62.9	37.1	30.3	5.9	0.9
65+	(80 880)	85.1	14.9	12.6	1.6	0.4
Quebec						
5-64	(5 632 045)	53.8	46.2	42.4	1.4	2.4
65+	(687 385)	77.6	22.4	21.2	0.4	0.8
Ontario						
5-64	(8 132 915)	48.4	51.6	42.5	3.2	5.9
65+	(1 092 785)	78.6	21.4	18.8	0.9	1.8
Manitoba						
5-64	(848 665)	52.8	47.2	39.4	5.0	2.8
65+	(135 460)	80.6	19.4	17.5	1.3	0.6
Saskatchewan						
5-64	(762 940)	57.3	42.7	36.9	4.7	1.1
65+	(128 320)	83.4	16.6	14.7	1.6	0.2
Alberta						
5-64	(2 082 710)	44.1	55.9	44.6	7.8	3.4
65+	(208 355)	77.8	22.2	17.3	3.3	1.6
British Columbia						
5-64	(2 618 610)	40.3	59.7	45.9	8.5	5.3
65+	(392 720)	67.7	32.3	26.5	3.8	1.9

Table 3.3: Five-Year Mobility Status, 1986-91, by Age and Province of Residence in 1991

Province of Residence and Age Group, 1991	Population 5+ Years of Age*	Non-movers	Total Movers	Intra-Provincial Movers	Inter-Provincial In-Migrants	Inter-National In-Migrants
	(n)	%	%	%	%	%
Yukon Territory						
5-64	(23 770)	34.4	65.6	36.9	26.8	1.8
65+	(1020)	59.3	41.2	31.8	7.8	1.5
Northwest Territories						
5-64	(47 925)	33.6	66.4	45.3	19.8	1.3
65+	(1475)	65.4	34.6	31.5	2.4	0.7

Source: see Table 3.2. Table 1A.
*Persons under five years of age are excluded because they did not have a previous residence five years earlier.

British Columbia also had the highest rate of in-migration of seniors from other countries during 1986-1991. Almost 2 in every 100 seniors resident in British Columbia in 1991 had arrived in the province from another country in the previous five years. Nevertheless, this high rate of international in-migration of seniors was counterbalanced by an even higher rate of international in-migration of non-seniors.

Table 3.4 shows the "five-year mobility status" of the population of British Columbia from 1986-1991 back to 1956-1961. The 1961 census was the first time that the five-year mobility question was asked. Table 3.4 shows that British Columbia has long attracted large numbers of senior and non-senior migrants from other provinces and other countries.

In 1996, almost half of British Columbians (49.2%) lived in the Vancouver Census Metropolitan Area. Table 3.4a shows the "five-year mobility status" of the population of the Vancouver CMA from 1986-1991 back to 1956-1961. It is apparent that Vancouver has long attracted senior and non-senior migrants from other provinces and other countries. In 1991, for example, almost 103 000 persons of all ages resident in Vancouver had come in the previous five years from other Canadian provinces, while almost 120 000 persons of all ages resident in Vancouver had come in the previous five years from other countries. In terms of the senior population in 1991, 2.4% of the seniors living in Vancouver (4400 seniors) had moved to the city in the previous five years from other Canadian provinces while another 2.9% (5200 seniors) had moved to Vancouver from other countries. This heavy in-migration of seniors to Vancouver contributes to population aging but is offset by even higher levels of in-migration of non-seniors.

In 1996, 8.2% of British Columbians lived in the Victoria Census Metropolitan Area. Table 3.4b shows the "five-year mobility status" of the population of the Victoria CMA from 1986-1991 back to 1956-1961. Victoria also has long attracted senior and non-senior migrants from other provinces and other countries. In 1991, for example, over 29 000 persons of all ages resident in Victoria had come in the previous five years from other Canadian provinces while almost 7000 persons resident in Victoria had come in the previous five years from other countries. In terms of the senior population in 1991, 5.9% of the seniors (3000) living in Victoria had moved to the city in the previous five years from other Canadian provinces, while another 1.5% (750 seniors) had moved to the city from other countries. This heavy in-migration of seniors to Victoria contributes to population aging but is offset by even higher levels of in-migration of non-seniors.

Table 3.4: Five-Year Mobility Status, 1956-1961 to 1986-1991 for the Province of British Columbia by Age and Year

Year and Age Group	Population	Non-Movers	Total Movers	Intra-Provincial Movers	Inter-Provincial In-Migrants	Inter-National In-Migrants	Not Stated
	%	%	%	%	%	%	%
1986-1991	**1991**						
5-64	(2 618 610)	40.3	59.7	45.9	8.5	5.3	n/a
65+	(392 720)	67.7	32.3	26.5	3.8	1.9	n/a
1981-1986	**1986**						
5-64	(2 318 040)	47.5	52.5	43.6	6.1	2.8	n/a
65+	(325 000)	73.7	26.3	21.8	2.8	1.8	n/a
1976-1981	**1981**						
5-64	(2 224 745)	40.4	59.6	45.8	9.9	3.9	n/a
65+	(276 215)	67.4	32.6	25.6	4.6	2.4	n/a
1971-1976	**1976**						
5-64	(2 049 355)	40.1	59.9	44.2	9.1	5.3	1.3
65+	(242 045)	61.0	39.0	30.5	4.1	2.1	2.3
1966-1971	**1971**						
5-64	(1 800 710)	40.8	59.2	40.7	10.2	6.1	2.2
65+	(205 150)	59.7	40.3	31.3	5.4	2.0	1.6
1956-1961	**1961**						
5-64	(1 215 541)	44.9	55.1	44.0	6.7	4.3	0.2
65+	(149 212)	65.3	34.7	29.7	3.9	1.0	0.1

Mobility data for 1961-1966 were not collected in the 1966 census.
Percentages may not add exactly to totals due to rounding.
Starting in 1981, values were imputed for non-response cases.
Sources: the data are adapted from the following: StatsCan. *Mobility and migration.* Ottawa: Industry, Science and Technology Canada, 1993. 1991 Census of Canada. Cat. #93-322, Table 1A; StatsCan. *Mobility status and interprovincial migration.* Ottawa: Supply and Services Canada, 1989. 1986 Census of Canada. Cat. #93-108, Table 2; StatsCan. *Mobility status.* Ottawa: Supply and Services Canada, 1983. 1981 Census of Canada. Cat. #92-907, Table 1; StatsCan. *Mobility status.* Ottawa: Supply

and Services Canada, 1978. 1976 Census of Canada. Cat. #92-828, Table 35;
StatsCan. *Internal Migration.* Ottawa: Industry, Trade and Commerce. 1971 Census
of Canada. Cat. #92-719, Table 31; Dominion Bureau of Statistics. *General charac-*
teristics of migrant and non-migrant population. Ottawa: Trade and Commerce. 1961
Census of Canada. Cat. #98-509, Table I1.

Table 3.4a: Five-Year Mobility Status, 1956-1961 to 1986-1991 for the Census
Metropolitan Area of Vancouver by Age and Year

Year and Age Group	Population	Non-Movers	Total Movers	Intra-Provincial Movers	Inter-Provincial In-Migrants	Inter-National In-Migrants	Not Stated
				Movers			
	%	%	%	%	%	%	%
1986-1991	1991						
5-64	(1 295 225)	38.3	61.7	45.3	7.6	8.8	n/a
65+	(180 120)	67.8	32.2	26.9	2.4	2.9	n/a
1976-1981	1981						
5-64	(1 039 700)	42.7	57.3	43.2	8.6	5.5	n/a
65+	(133 015)	68.9	31.1	24.7	3.1	3.3	n/a
1971-1976	1976						
5-64	(970 005)	42.8	57.2	40.7	7.7	7.4	1.4
65+	(123 160)	61.9	38.1	30.3	2.5	2.6	2.8
1956-1961	1961						
5-64	(591 771)	45.0	55.0	43.0	6.4	5.4	0.1
65+	(77 627)	64.2	35.8	31.3	3.3	1.1	0.1

Data for the Vancouver CMA were not available for 1981-86, 1966-71 or 1961-66.
Percentages may not add exactly to totals due to rounding.
Starting in 1981, values were imputed for non-response cases.
Sources for table 3.4a and 3.4b: the data are adapted from the following: StatsCan.
Mobility and migration. Ottawa: Industry, Science and Technology Canada, 1993.
1991 Census of Canada. Cat. #93-322, Table 1C; StatsCan. *Mobility status.* Ottawa:
Supply and Services Canada, 1983. 1981 Census of Canada. Cat. #92-907, Table 3;
StatsCan. *Mobility status.* Ottawa: Supply and Services Canada, 1978. 1976 Census
of Canada. Cat. #92-828, Table 37; Dominion Bureau of Statistics. *Characteristics*
of migrant and non-migrant population, Metropolitan areas. Ottawa: Trade and
Commerce. 1961 Census of Canada. Cat. #98-529, Bulletin SX-15, Table 1.

Table 3.4b: Five-Year Mobility Status, 1956-1961 to 1986-1991 for the Census Metropolitan Area of Victoria by Age and Year

Year and Age Group	Population	Non-Movers	Total Movers	Intra-Provincial Movers	Inter-Provincial In-Migrants	Inter-National In-Migrants	Not Stated
	%	%	%	%	%	%	%
1986-1991	1991						
5-64	(215 070)	38.2	61.8	46.9	12.2	2.7	n/a
65+	(50 065)	68.5	31.5	24.1	5.9	1.5	n/a
1976-1981	1981						
5-64	(179 970)	40.5	59.5	43.4	12.9	3.2	n/a
65+	(36 715)	65.7	34.3	25.4	6.9	2.1	n/a
1971-1976	1976						
5-64	(172 155)	39.1	60.9	43.3	12.3	4.2	1.1
65+	(33 735)	56.8	43.2	32.2	7.0	2.0	2.1
1956-1961	1961						
5-64	(107 564)	43.6	56.4	44.0	8.2	4.1	0.1
65+	(22 027)	62.3	37.7	30.4	5.7	1.5	0.1

Data for the Victoria CMA were not available for 1981-86, 1966-71 or 1961-66. See Table 3.4a for notes and sources.

Table 3.5: Interprovincial Migration in Canada, 1990-91

Province of Residence 1990	Newfoundland N[1]	Newfoundland E[1]	Prince Edward Island N	Prince Edward Island E	Nova Scotia N	Nova Scotia E	New Brunswick N	New Brunswick E	Quebec N	Quebec E	Ontario N	Ontario E
Newfoundland	-	-	80	0	1795	85	640	15	400	10	4790	50
Prince Edward Island	120	0	-	-	980	65	315	10	140	10	645	10
Nova Scotia	1080	20	575	15	-	-	2760	55	1035	70	7175	715
New Brunswick	450	15	520	10	2575	75	-	-	2040	75	4090	150
Quebec	340	10	100	10	980	30	2090	70	-	-	21,465	1230
Ontario	6530	90	855	40	7285	190	4680	105	18,000	480	-	-
Manitoba	280	0	5	10	680	10	325	25	815	10	4880	175
Saskatchewan	70	0	0	0	285	10	95	0	195	25	2520	100
Alberta	780	10	260	10	1475	10	1090	0	1950	30	9055	260
British Columbia	420	10	40	0	1550	60	575	25	2045	60	9970	430
Yukon Territory	25	0	0	0	45	0	10	0	35	0	230	0
Northwest Territories	180	0	0	0	110	0	70	0	145	0	530	0
Total In-Migrants	10,275	155	2435	95	17,765	535	12,650	305	26,800	770	65,350	2580
Index of Dissimilarity[2]	13.3		23.8		15.3		16.7		11.3		16.4	
Net Migration	-120	-50	-405	0	80	100	295	-100	-6960	-840	-21,650	-240

1. N = nonelderly 1-64 years of age; E = elderly 65+ years of age.
2. ID = ½ $\sum |N-E|$ where N and E are %s of total in-migrants.

Source: Adapted from Statistics Canada Mobility and migration. Ottawa: Industry, Science and Technology, Canada 1993. 1991 Census of Canada, Catalogue Number 93-322. Table 2B (20% sample, excludes persons institutionalized in previous six or more months)

The above discussion of migration focuses on persons who have moved recently to British Columbia. Of course, at the same time that some people are moving to the province, others are moving out of the province. With regard to interprovincial migration in Canada in 1990-1991, Table 3.5 shows that British Columbia gained 3285 seniors from other provinces while losing 1690 seniors for a net gain of 1595 seniors. British Columbia had by far the largest net gain of seniors of any Canadian province in 1990-1991. In that same year, British Columbia had a net gain of 35 790 non-seniors from other Canadian provinces, by far the largest net gain of non-seniors of any Canadian province in 1990-1991.

Table 3.5 also shows that the in-migration streams of senior and non-senior interprovincial migrants coming to British Columbia in 1990-1991 were very similar. Indeed, the senior and non-senior streams were more similar for British Columbia than for any other province. As a result, the senior and non-senior in-migration streams to British Columbia from other provinces tend to have counterbalancing impacts on population aging in that province.

Table 3.6 shows interprovincial migration in Canada over the five-year period from 1986 to 1991. During this period of time, British Columbia gained 14 995 seniors from other provinces while losing 5770 seniors for a net gain of 9225 seniors. British Columbia had by far the largest net gain of seniors of any Canadian province in 1986-1991. In that same period of time, British Columbia had a net gain of 116 645 non-seniors from other Canadian provinces, by far the largest net gain of non-seniors of any Canadian province in 1986-1991.

Manitoba		Saskatchewan		Alberta		British Columbia		Yukon Territory		Northwest Territories		Total Out-Migrants	
N	E	N	E	N	E	N	E	N	E	N	E	N	E
405	10	95	0	1205	0	730	25	90	10	165	0	10,395	205
20	0	40	0	315	0	230	0	10	0	25	0	2840	95
555	25	145	0	1935	25	2170	50	60	0	195	0	17,685	435
430	10	175	0	1135	30	870	40	10	0	60	0	12,355	405
670	10	305	10	2800	45	4805	185	20	0	185	10	33,760	1610
5620	130	2865	100	16,990	490	23,335	1175	255	10	585	10	87,000	2820
-	-	2430	100	4935	100	5870	315	125	10	225	0	20,570	755
2445	100	-	-	13,375	265	6805	445	130	0	340	10	26,260	955
3395	75	7400	140	-	-	27,160	990	365	0	1085	0	54,015	1525
2370	185	2890	145	16,925	750	-	-	715	25	465	0	37,965	1690
70	0	135	0	340	0	890	30	-	-	65	0	1845	30
200	0	330	10	1350	0	890	30	125	0	-	-	3930	40
16,180	545	16,810	505	61,305	1705	73,755	3285	1905	55	3395	30	308,625	10,565
23.7		19.8		17.5		10.1		37.8		67.3			
-4390	-210	-9450	-450	7290	180	35,790	1595	60	25	-535	-10		

Table 3.6: Interprovincial Migration in Canada, 1986-91

Province of Residence 1986	Newfoundland		Prince Edward Island		Nova Scotia		New Brunswick		Quebec		Ontario	
	N[1]	E[1]	N	E	N	E	N	E	N	E	N	E
Newfoundland	-	-	530	0	6100	150	1655	30	750	20	17,885	205
Prince Edward Island	195	0	-	-	2195	125	1490	45	955	25	3045	90
Nova Scotia	3040	70	2035	75	-	-	7695	205	3885	130	25,810	675
New Brunswick	1140	30	1150	40	8575	370	-	-	6315	250	15,690	440
Quebec	1930	45	470	40	3020	230	6110	375	-	-	68,270	4510
Ontario	9190	255	2440	165	18,785	1085	10,890	525	49,420	2010	-	-
Manitoba	625	0	290	0	1865	15	1065	20	3825	120	22,430	650
Saskatchewan	230	20	180	0	790	15	595	15	1740	80	13,655	300
Alberta	2450	20	960	45	5290	30	3025	45	6365	135	54,630	1015
British Columbia	1195	20	285	10	3895	85	1795	50	5335	195	36,320	1425
Yukon Territory	10	0	0	0	25	10	50	0	110	0	830	0
Northwest Territories	260	10	70	0	595	0	150	0	330	0	2070	40
Total In-Migrants	20,265	470	8410	375	51,135	2115	34,520	1310	79,030	2965	260,635	935
Index of Dissimilarity[2]	13.8		20.6		22.3		19.6		6.2		23.3	
Net Migration	-13,890	-55	-900	50	-5420	535	-5980	-80	-21,940	-3620	49,895	-293

1. N = nonelderly 5-64 years of age; E = elderly 65+ years of age.
2. ID = ½ $\sum$ |N-E| where N and E are %s of total in-migrants.

Source: Adapted from Statistics Canada *Mobility and migration*. Ottawa: Industry, Science and Technology, Canada 1993. 1991 Census of Canada. Catalogue Number 93-322. Table 2A (20% sample, excludes persons institutionalized in previous six or more months)

Table 3.6 also shows that the in-migration streams of senior and non-senior interprovincial migrants coming to British Columbia in 1986-1991 were quite similar. Indeed, the senior and non-senior streams were more similar for British Columbia than all other provinces except Quebec and Newfoundland. As a result, the interprovincial senior and non-senior in-migration streams to British Columbia tend to have counterbalancing impacts on population aging in that province.

Table 3.7 shows that British Columbia has consistently gained over the years from the net migration of both seniors and non-seniors coming from other Canadian provinces. While the net migration gain of Canadian seniors moving to British Columbia has contributed over the years to population aging in that province, the net migration gain of non-seniors moving from other Canadian provinces has tended to counterbalance the aging trend.

The above discussion ignores the out-migration of seniors and non-seniors from British Columbia to other countries. Because people are free to leave Canada without notifying Canadian authorities, international out-migration is known only indirectly by solving the following formula:

$$\text{population size at time2} = \text{population size at time1} + (\text{births - deaths}) + (\text{in-migrants - out-migrants})$$

Manitoba		Saskatchewan		Alberta		British Columbia		Yukon Territory		Northwest Territories		Total Out-Migrants	
N	E	N	E	N	E	N	E	N	E	N	E	N	E
840	0	280	0	3080	35	2455	75	165	10	415	0	34,155	525
95	0	170	0	640	10	420	30	25	0	80	0	9310	325
1295	45	675	15	5650	130	5815	235	140	0	515	0	56,555	1580
1200	30	575	0	3115	80	2475	150	55	0	210	0	40,500	1390
1885	65	940	40	7015	465	10,685	815	140	0	505	0	100,970	6585
12,280	590	5985	380	37,340	1670	62,240	5590	770	10	1400	0	210,740	12,280
-	-	7105	390	16,640	485	20,610	1900	410	15	845	10	75,710	3605
9095	255	-	-	42,790	1235	24,335	1715	390	10	1135	10	94,935	3655
9370	205	13,965	535	-	-	88,220	4360	1350	15	2985	10	188,610	6415
5595	545	5800	650	42,520	2755	-	-	2500	25	1290	10	106,530	5770
90	0	105	10	1055	35	3150	75	-	-	115	0	5540	130
565	10	590	15	3190	85	2770	50	430	0	-	-	11,020	210
42,310	1745	36,190	2035	163,035	6985	223,175	14,995	6375	85	9495	40	934,575	42,470
22.8		18.3		16.8		14.0		26.1		40.5			
-33,400	-1860	-58,745	-1620	-25,575	570	116,645	9225	835	-45	-1525	-170		

Table 3.7: Net Interprovincial Migration, for British Columbia, 1956-1961 to 1986-1991

Period	Non-elderly Ages 5-64	Elderly Ages 65+
1986-1991	116 645	9240
1981-1986	5460	4035
1976-1981	102 600	8330
1971-1976	89 760	6130
1966-1971	All ages: 120 035	
1961-1966	No Data	No Data
1956-1961	29 645	3585

Mobility data for 1961-1966 were not collected in the 1966 census.
Sources: the data are adapted from the following: StatsCan. *Mobility and migration.* Ottawa: Industry, Science and Technology Canada, 1993. 1991 Census of Canada. Cat. #93-322, Table 2A; StatsCan. *Mobility status and interprovincial migration.* Ottawa: Supply and Services Canada, 1989. 1986 Census of Canada. Cat. #93-108, Table 4B; StatsCan. *Mobility status.* Ottawa: Supply and Services Canada, 1983. 1981 Census of Canada. Cat. #92-907, Table 1; StatsCan. *Mobility status.* Ottawa: Supply and Services Canada, 1978. 1976 Census of Canada. Cat. #92-828, Table 36; StatsCan. *Internal migration.* Ottawa: Industry, Trade and Commerce. 1971 Census of Canada. Cat. #92-719, Tables 31 and 32; Dominion Bureau of Statistics. *General*

characteristics of migrant and non-migrant population. Ottawa: Trade and Commerce. 1961 Census of Canada. Cat. #98-509, Table I4.

All but the international out-migration component of this formula are available from the Canadian Censuses or from Canadian Vital Statistics. In other words, this formula can be used to assess the number of international out-migrants, although it cannot tell us to which countries these migrants have gone. Table 3.8 shows estimates of net interprovincial and net international migration for British Columbia for 1991-1992 through 1994-1995. International in-migration streams are estimated to be far greater than international out-migration streams resulting in substantial net gains for both non-seniors and seniors in British Columbia.

Table 3.8: Postcensal Estimates of Net Interprovincial and Net International Migration, British Columbia 1991-1995

Year and Age Group		Interprovincial Migration			International Migration		
		In	Out	Net	In	Out	Net
1994-95							
	0-64	84 257	52 120	32 137	42 474	6772	35 702
	65+	3285	3010	275	2096	264	1832
1993-94							
	0-64	76 523	37 956	38 567	45 952	6607	39 345
	65+	3005	2195	810	2011	257	1754
1992-93							
	0-64	72 424	34 740	37 684	38 688	6488	32 200
	65+	2700	1999	701	1978	252	1726
1991-92							
	0-64	80 447	44 116	36 331	32 400	6793	25 607
	65+	3508	2445	1063	1672	224	1448

Sources: StatsCan, 1996. Annual Demographic Statistics, 1995. Cat. #91-213-XPB. Annual. Tables 4.16-4.17, 4.20-4.22. StatsCan, 1995. Annual Demographic Statistics, 1994. Cat. #91-213. Annual. Tables 4.16-4.17, 4.20-4.22. StatsCan, 1994. Annual Demographic Statistics, 1993. Cat. #91-213. Annual. Tables 4.16-4.17, 4.19-4.21.

British Columbia "is the only province that has grown at a faster rate than the national average in every Census since Confederation" (Statistics Canada, 1997b:3). Indeed, "British Columbia had the fastest growth rate of the 10 provinces between 1986 and 1991, and 1991 and 1996. International migration accounted for about 45% of B.C.'s rapid growth, interprovincial migration 35%, and natural increase [births minus deaths] the [remaining 20%]" (Statistics Canada, 1997b:3). Vancouver, Canada's third largest census metropolitan area, was the fastest growing CMA in 1991-96 increasing 14.3% in population (Statistics Canada, 1997b:4). British Columbia's rapid rate of growth has meant that the province's share of the national population has increased over the years from 1.0% in 1871, the year British Columbia entered Confederation, to 6.0%

in 1921, 8.7% in 1956, and 12.9% in 1996 (Burke, 1994:314; also calculated from Statistics Canada, 1992 and Statistics Canada, 1997b).

Table 3.9 shows the rates of population increase for Canada's provinces from 1951 to 1996 and Table 3.9a compares the rates of increase for seniors and non-seniors. The senior population grows as a result of persons turning age 65 (aging in place) minus deaths of persons 65 and older plus the in-migration of seniors minus the out-migration of seniors. Differential rates of growth of the senior and non-senior populations have implications for the population aging trend. More specifically, if the senior population grows faster than the non-senior population, then the population will age.

As noted above, British Columbia has had a faster rate of growth than Canada as a whole. Table 3.9 shows relevant data for the 1951 to 1996 period. Not only has British Columbia grown at a faster rate than the Canadian average, it has also tended to grow at a faster rate than any other province. In the five-year periods from 1951 to 1996, British Columbia ranked first six times out of nine in terms of rate of growth (including one tie with Alberta). In the other three time periods, British Columbia was second to Alberta twice and third once behind Alberta and Ontario.

In order to determine whether the senior population or the non-senior population is growing faster, Table 3.9a shows the growth rates for seniors and non-seniors for Canada and British Columbia from 1951 to 1996. For Canada as a whole, the non-senior population grew at a faster rate from 1951 to 1961 than the senior population, reflecting the baby boom phenomenon. Subsequently, from 1961 to 1996, the senior population has consistently grown at a faster rate than the non-senior population, reflecting the aging of the Canadian population. For British Columbia, the non-senior population grew at a faster rate than the senior population from 1951 to 1971 and again from 1991 to 1996. In the intervening years from 1971 to 1991, the senior population grew at a faster rate than the non-senior population, allowing British Columbia to "age" during this time. Nevertheless, British Columbia's aging trend has been less consistent than the Canadian trend over the last half century, largely because of the province's attraction for non-senior in-migrants from other provinces and from other countries.

Table 3.9: Rates of Population Increase for Canada and the Provinces, 1951-1996

| Province | Percent Change in Population Total | | | | | | | | |
	1991-96 %	1986-91 %	1981-86 %	1976-81 %	1971-76 %	1966-71 %	1961-66 %	1956-61 %	1951-56 %
CANADA	5.7	7.9	4.0	5.9	6.6	7.8	9.7	13.4	14.8
British Columbia	13.5	13.8	5.1	11.3	12.9	16.6	15.0	16.5	20.0
Alberta	5.9	7.6	5.7	21.7	12.9	11.3	9.9	18.6	19.5
Saskatchewan	0.1	-2.0	4.3	5.1	-0.5	-3.0	3.3	5.1	5.9

Table 3.9: Rates of Population Increase for Canada and the Provinces, 1951-1996

Province	Percent Change in Population Total								
	1991-96 %	1986-91 %	1981-86 %	1976-81 %	1971-76 %	1966-71 %	1961-66 %	1956-61 %	1951-56 %
Manitoba	2.0	2.7	3.6	0.5	3.4	2.6	4.5	8.4	9.5
Ontario	6.6	10.8	5.5	4.4	7.3	10.7	11.6	15.4	17.6
Quebec	3.5	5.6	1.5	3.3	3.4	4.3	9.9	13.6	14.1
New Brunswick	2.0	2.0	1.9	2.8	6.7	2.9	3.2	7.8	7.5
Nova Scotia	1.0	3.1	3.0	2.3	5.0	4.4	2.6	6.1	8.1
Prince Edward Island	3.7	2.5	3.4	3.6	5.9	2.9	3.7	5.4	0.9
Newfoundland	-2.9	0.0	0.1	1.8	6.8	5.8	7.8	10.3	14.8
Yukon Territory	10.7	18.3	1.5	6.0	18.7	27.9	-1.7	20.0	34.0
Northwest Territories	11.7	10.4	14.2	7.3	22.4	21.1	25.0	19.1	20.7

$$\text{Rate of Increase for Time}_t = \frac{(\text{Population at Time}_t - \text{Population at Time}_{t-1})}{\text{Population at Time}_{t-1}} \times 100$$

where t is a census year and $t-1$ is the census year five years previous

Sources: Calculated from StatsCan., 1997. 1996 Census of Canada – Population and Dwelling Counts. *The Daily*, April 15, 1997. Cat. #11-001E (for 1996); StatsCan., 1992. 1991 Census of Canada, Age, Sex and Marital Status. Cat. #93-310, Table 1. Ottawa: Supply and Services Canada (for 1951 to 1991).

Table 3.9a: Percent Change in the Size of Senior and Non-Senior Populations for British Columbia and Canada, 1951-1996

Province and Age Group	1991-96 %	1986-91 %	1981-86 %	1976-81 %	1971-76 %	1966-71 %	1961-66 %	1956-61 %	1951-56 %
Canada									
65+	11.3	17.5	14.3	17.9	14.8	13.3	10.7	11.8	14.5
0-64	4.9	6.7	2.9	4.7	5.9	7.3	9.7	13.5	14.8
British Columbia									
+65	12.8	20.8	17.2	23.2	18.1	14.7	7.9	9.8	19.5
0-64	13.6	12.9	3.6	10.0	12.4	16.8	15.8	17.3	20.1

Sources: see Table 3.9

In the 1991 to 1996 period of time, British Columbia attracted one out of every five immigrants of all ages coming to Canada (Statistics Canada, 1997c:6). Furthermore, Table 3.10 shows that well over one-third of seniors living in British Columbia in 1991 had been born in another country. Indeed, Table 3.10

shows that only 20% of British Columbia's seniors in 1991 had been born in that province, 43% had been born in other provinces, and 37% in other countries. Table 3.10a shows the national origins of seniors resident in the province in 1991 who had immigrated from another country at some earlier time in their lives. Of those seniors born in other countries, 36% were born in the United Kingdom, 35% in other European countries, 17% originated in Asia, 8% in the United States, and 1% in each of Oceania, Africa and Central/South America. Note that these statistics apply only to those seniors who have immigrated at some time in their lives to British Columbia from other countries. Turning to all seniors – both immigrant and non-immigrant – resident in British Columbia in 1991, seniors who had been born in the United Kingdom made up 13% of all seniors in the province while other European immigrants made up another 13% of all seniors. Immigrants from Asia and the United States made up 6% and 3% respectively of all seniors in British Columbia.

Table 3.10: Place of Birth for Seniors Living in British Columbia in 1991

Place of Birth	Number	Percentage of all Seniors
Born in Canada		
British Columbia	79 275	20.2
Other Provinces in Canada	167 670	42.7
Born Outside Canada		
Canadian Born	1615	0.4
Other Country (Immigrants)	144 100	36.7
TOTAL	392 660	100.0

Source: Adapted from StatsCan. *Immigration and Citizenship*. Ottawa: Supply and Services Canada, 1992. 1991 Census of Canada. Cat. #93-316. Table 4. (20% sample, excludes persons institutionalized 6+ months).

Table 3.10a: Place of Birth for Immigrant Seniors Living in British Columbia in 1991

Place of Birth	Number	Percentage of all Seniors	Percentage of Immigrant Seniors
USA	11 775	3.0	8.2
Central and South America	1345	0.3	0.9
Europe			
Germany	8225	2.1	5.7
Italy	4580	1.2	3.2
Netherlands	5460	1.4	3.8
Poland	5605	1.4	3.9
Scandinavia	6650	1.7	4.6
United Kingdom	51 925	13.2	36.0
USSR	7900	2.0	5.5
Other Europe	12 345	3.1	8.6
Africa	1440	0.4	1.0
Asia			
Hong Kong	1385	0.4	1.0
Japan	930	0.2	0.6
China (PDRC)	12 240	3.1	8.5
Philippines	1985	0.5	1.4
India	5225	1.3	3.6
Other Asia	3055	0.8	2.1
Oceania and Other	2015	0.5	1.4
TOTAL	144 085	36.6	100.0

Totals in Tables 3.10 and 3.10a do not match exactly due to rounding.
Source: see Table 3.10.

This pattern of ethnic origins for seniors in British Columbia will change in time given current patterns of immigration. In 1991-1996, some 217 000 persons of all ages immigrated to British Columbia from other countries. Of these, 21% were from Hong Kong, 13% from the People's Republic of China, 11% from Taiwan, 10% from India, 7% from the Philippines, and 3% each from South Korea, the United Kingdom and the United States (Statistics Canada, 1996-1997). In time, the aging of these immigrants will create a senior population that has a different ethnic composition than the senior population at present.

The census metropolitan area of Vancouver received 18% of all immigrants of all ages coming to Canada during the 1991-1996 period and 88% of all immigrants of all ages coming to British Columbia during the 1991-1996 period. Eighty percent (80%) of these immigrants coming to Vancouver were Asian-born. "Immigrants accounted for over a third (35%) of Vancouver's population in 1996, making it the census metropolitan area with the second largest immigrant population [second to Toronto]. . . . Nearly one-fifth (19%) of Vancouver's total population consisted of immigrants who came to Canada since 1981." (Statistics Canada, 1997c:1-2, 6). In 1991-1996, some 190 000 persons of all ages immigrated to Vancouver from other countries. Of these, 24% were from Hong Kong, 14% from the People's Republic of China, 12% from Taiwan, 9% from India, 7% from the Philippines, and 3% from South Korea (Statistics Canada, 1997c:6). In time, the aging of these immigrants will create a senior population in Vancouver that has a different ethnic composition than the senior population at present.

This chapter has examined trends in fertility, mortality and migration in British Columbia. These trends have determined the aging of the population in the province. In general, declining fertility and decreasing mortality have contributed to population aging. While the in-migration of seniors from other Canadian provinces and from other countries has also contributed to population aging in British Columbia, in general, the in-migration of non-seniors from other Canadian provinces and from other countries has had a counterbalancing effect.

The impact of the growing population of seniors is often assessed by calculating the ratio of the seniors population to the population of working age — the so-called dependency ratio. The impact of the seniors population is also assessed, in part, by focusing on the demographic characteristics of the seniors population. The next chapter examines trends in the dependency ratio and presents a demographic profile of seniors in British Columbia.

Chapter Four
The Demographic Characteristics of Seniors in British Columbia

This chapter examines selected demographic characteristics of seniors in British Columbia. More specifically, this chapter discusses trends in the so-called dependency ratio and also examines marital status, living arrangements, labor force activity and socio-economic status (income and education).

Table 4.1 shows the dependency ratios for Canada's provinces in 1996. The seniors dependency ratio indicates the number of persons 65 years of age and older per 100 persons 15 to 64 years of age. The youth dependency ratio indicates the number of persons 14 years of age and younger per 100 persons 15 to 64 years of age. These dependency ratios are a very crude indicator of the number of "dependent" persons (young and old) in the population per 100 "independent" persons (of working age). In other words, these dependency ratios provide a crude measure of taxpayer "burden." As dependency ratios rise, the burden on the taxpayer tends to rise. As dependency ratios fall, the burden on the taxpayer tends to fall. For example, an increasing seniors dependency ratio implies increasing costs for old age income security, health care, long-term care and seniors' housing. A decreasing youth dependency ratio implies decreasing costs for family income security, education and policing.

Table 4.1 shows that in 1996, British Columbia's youth dependency ratio was a little lower than the Canadian average, while the province's seniors dependency ratio was a little higher than the Canadian average. British Columbia's overall dependency ratio – the sum of the youth and seniors dependency ratios – was a little lower than the Canadian average. Unlike Saskatchewan, for example, British Columbia has a population age structure, as measured by the dependency ratios, that is quite "typical" for a Canadian province in 1996. While British Columbia stands out among Canadian provinces in terms of its attraction for migrants from other parts of Canada and from other countries, nevertheless, migration patterns have not "distorted" British Columbia's age structure.

British Columbia's dependency ratios have changed over the years. Table 4.2 shows trends in the province's youth and seniors dependency ratios from 1921 to 1996. The youth dependency ratio fell from 1921 to 1941, rose during the baby boom years and then trended downward again from the early 1960s to 1996. The seniors dependency ratio rose from 1921 to 1956, declined up to 1976 as the baby boom reached working age and then rose again up until 1991. From 1991 to 1996, the seniors dependency ratio declined under the influence of heavy in-migration of non-seniors. Whether or not this recent downward trend will continue remains to be seen.

Table 4.1: Dependency Ratios for Canada, by Province, 1996

Province	Overall Dependency Ratio	Youth Dependency Ratio	Seniors Dependency Ratio
British Columbia	48.2	29.2	18.9
Alberta	48.5	33.8	14.7
Saskatchewan	60.7	37.1	23.6
Manitoba	55.3	34.1	21.2
Ontario	49.2	30.7	18.5
Quebec	45.5	28.0	17.5
New Brunswick	47.5	28.9	18.6
Nova Scotia	48.6	29.5	19.0
Prince Edward Island	52.9	33.1	19.8
Newfoundland	44.2	28.7	15.5
Yukon Territory	39.7	33.5	6.2
Northwest Territories	55.3	50.6	4.7
CANADA	48.6	30.4	18.2

Source: Calculated from www.statcan.ca, 1996 Census bin. Population by Selected Age Groups and Sex for Canada, Provinces and Territories. 1996 Census (100% data). Accessed Dec. 19, 1997.

Youth dependency ratio = $\frac{\text{\# 0-14 years of age}}{\text{\# 15-64 years of age}}$ x 100

Seniors dependency ratio = $\frac{\text{\# 65+ years of age}}{\text{\# 15-64 years of age}}$ x 100

Overall dependency ratio = Youth dependency ratio + Seniors dependency ratio

While the overall dependency ratio (youth and seniors combined) declined somewhat in British Columbia from 1921 to 1941, it rose from 1941 to 1961 and then declined up to 1981, levelling off through 1996 at a level only slightly above the 1921 to 1941 period. The separate trends in the youth and seniors dependency ratios have tended to have a counterbalancing effect on trends in the overall dependency ratio.

Table 4.2: Dependency Ratios for British Columbia, 1921-1996

Year	Overall Dependency Ratio	Youth Dependency Ratio	Seniors Dependency Ratio
1921	47.1	41.9	5.2
1931	43.2	35.3	7.9
1941	42.3	30.5	11.8
1951	58.6	41.4	17.2
1956	66.1	48.2	17.9
1961	70.7	53.4	17.4
1966	67.2	51.2	15.9
1971	59.5	44.5	15.0
1976	51.4	36.5	14.9
1981	47.7	31.7	16.0
1986	48.4	30.4	18.0
1991	49.3	30.1	19.2
1996	48.2	29.2	18.9

Source: for 1921-1991: Calculated from StatsCan, 1992. 1991 Census of Canada. Age, Sex and Marital Status. Cat. #93-310, Table 1. For 1996: see Table 4.1.

Table 4.3 shows the projected trends in the youth and seniors dependency ratios for British Columbia from 1996 to 2016 under various assumptions about population growth rates. The youth dependency ratio is projected to decline regardless of whether growth rates are low, medium or high. However, the greatest decline in the youth dependency ratio is expected with a low growth rate. In contrast, the seniors dependency ratio is projected to *increase* regardless of whether growth rates are low, medium or high. In this case, however, a low growth rate produces the greatest increase in the seniors dependency ratio. Similarly, the median age of the population is expected to increase regardless of whether growth rates are low, medium or high. Further, the greatest increase in the median age of the population is expected with a low growth rate. In short, it is projected that the population of British Columbia will age as the youth dependency ratio decreases and the seniors dependency ratio increases during the 1996 to 2016 period of time. This aging trend will be most pronounced with relatively low growth rates and less pronounced under high rates of growth.

Table 4.3 also shows the overall dependency ratios (youth and seniors combined). During the 1996 to 2016 period of time in British Columbia, the overall dependency ratio is projected to first decline and then rise. The overall dependency ratio in 2016 will be lowest if growth rates are low. In any case, the overall dependency ratio in 2016 is not projected to be substantially different from 1996.

Table 4.3: Projected Dependency Ratios and Median Age for British Columbia, 1996-2016

Projection	1996	2001	2006	2011	2016
Youth Dependency Ratio					
1. Low Growth	29.0	26.7	24.2	22.4	22.1
2. Medium Growth	29.2	27.5	25.9	24.8	24.7
3. High Growth[1]	29.5	28.6	27.9	27.5	27.4
Seniors Dependency Ratio					
1. Low Growth	19.4	19.5	19.8	21.2	24.7
2. Medium Growth	19.4	19.5	19.7	21.0	24.2
3. High Growth	19.4	19.3	19.4	20.6	23.6
Overall Dependency Ratio					
1. Low Growth	48.4	46.2	44.0	43.6	46.8
2. Medium Growth	48.6	47.0	45.6	45.8	48.9
3. High Growth	48.9	47.9	47.3	48.1	51.0
Median Age					
1. Low Growth	35.9	37.6	39.3	40.7	41.9
2. Medium Growth	35.9	37.4	38.7	39.9	40.7
3. High Growth	35.7	37.0	37.9	38.7	39.5

[1]High growth and west internal migration.
Source: Adapted from StatsCan., 1994. Population Projections for Canada, Provinces and Territories 1993-2016. Ottawa: Minister of Industry, Science and Technology. Table A3.

Turning to demographic characteristics, Table 4.4 shows the marital status of seniors in British Columbia in 1996. Relatively small percentages of seniors have never been married. Even smaller percentages of seniors in 1996 were currently separated. Among seniors, males were somewhat more likely than females to be currently separated. Furthermore, younger seniors were more likely than older seniors to be currently separated. Similarly, younger seniors were more likely than older seniors to be currently divorced. However, female seniors tended to be somewhat more likely than male seniors to be currently divorced. These data suggest that separation and divorce are becoming increasingly common and that increasing percentages of seniors can be expected in the future to be either separated or divorced.

Most people marry at some time in their lives and the majority of males who were 65 to 89 years of age in British Columbia in 1996 were currently married. The majority of females who were seniors 65 to 74 years of age were also currently married. However, the probability of being currently married decreases with increasing age, and a majority of men aged 90 and older, along with a majority of women aged 75 and older, were not currently married, primarily due to the death of their spouses. Indeed, the chances of being currently widowed increase with increasing age and are much greater for women than for men. In 1996 in British Columbia, some 5% of males aged 65 to 69 were widowed, while 22% of women of the same age were widowed. In comparison, 46% of men aged 90 and older were widowed, while 86% of women aged 90 and older were widowed. Women are much more likely than men to be currently widowed and much less likely to be currently married because men tend to be older than their wives and have a shorter life expectancy. In other words, for any given couple, the husband is more likely to die before the wife.

Table 4.4: Marital Status of Seniors in British Columbia, by Age and Sex, 1996

Marital Status	Age					
	65-69 %	70-74 %	75-79 %	80-84 %	85-89 %	90+ %
Never Married						
Males	5.4	4.8	4.2	4.2	4.6	6.6
Females	3.5	3.6	4.0	4.9	5.4	6.6
Currently Married (or Common Law)						
Males	80.5	79.2	76.3	69.5	59.0	43.5
Females	63.2	53.4	40.9	26.6	15.4	5.7
Separated						
Males	2.5	2.4	2.1	2.0	2.1	1.6
Females	2.3	2.0	1.6	1.3	0.8	0.5
Widowed						
Males	5.2	8.5	13.5	21.2	31.8	46.2
Females	22.4	34.2	48.2	63.8	76.0	85.8
Divorced						
Males	6.4	5.1	3.8	3.1	2.5	2.1
Females	8.6	6.7	5.2	3.5	2.3	1.4
TOTALS[1]						
Males (%)	100.0	100.0	99.9	100.0	100.0	100.0
Males (n)	64 720	49 280	36 190	19 720	8895	3550
Females (%)	100.0	99.9	99.9	100.1	99.9	100.0
Females (n)	74 085	62 000	48 675	30 175	15 800	8930

[1]Totals may not add to 100.0% due to rounding.
Source: Adapted from StatsCan., 1997. The Nation Series, Edition 1 (StatsCan. Cat. #9350020XCB96001). 1996 Census of Canada (CD-ROM). Ottawa: Minister of Industry.

Table 4.5 shows the living arrangements of seniors in British Columbia in 1991. For seniors 65 to 74 years of age, the great majority of both males and females live with others (usually their spouse) in private households. Nevertheless, males are more likely than females to live with another person or persons in a private household (84% of males 65 to 74 years of age versus 68% of females). Females are more likely to live alone (29% of females aged 65 to 74 versus 13% of males). Very few seniors in this age group reside in hospitals or in special care homes for the elderly and chronically ill.

The probabilities of living alone or residing in hospitals or special care homes increase with increasing age, while the probability of living in a private household declines. Nevertheless, the majority of males 75 or more years of age live with others (usually their spouse) in private households. Indeed, males 75 or more years of age are more likely than females to live with another person or persons in a private household (72% of males 75 or more years of age versus 41% of their female counterparts). Females are more likely to live alone (43% of females aged 75 and older versus 19% of their male counterparts). Relatively few seniors in this age group reside in hospitals (1.2% of females and 0.8% of males). The most striking contrast between the older and younger seniors is the increased likelihood of residing in special care homes for the elderly and chronically ill. In 1991, 7.6% of males and 14.5% of females 75 years of age and older lived in special care homes in comparison to 1.2% of males and 1.4% of females 65 to 74 years of age.

Table 4.5: Numbers and Percentages of Seniors Residing in Private Households and in Hospitals and Special Care Homes in British Columbia in 1991, by Age and Sex

Living Arrangement	65-74				75+			
	Males		Females		Males		Females	
	#	%	#	%	#	%	#	%
Living with others in Private Households	95 820	84.1	93 110	68.4	49 065	71.8	42 325	40.9
Living Alone	15 210	13.3	39 390	28.9	12 870	18.8	44 040	42.5
In Hospitals[1]	355	0.3	330	0.2	575	0.8	1245	1.2
In Special Care Homes[2]	1370	1.2	1960	1.4	5170	7.6	15 015	14.5

[1]General hospitals, psychiatric hospitals and hospitals for the physically handicapped.
[2]Special care homes for the elderly and chronically ill.
Source: StatsCan., 1992. 1991 Census of Canada. Families: Number, Type and Structure. Cat. #93-312, Table 8. Dwellings and Households. Cat. #93-311, Table 2. Percentages calculated using totals from Age, Sex and Marital Status. Cat. #93-310, Table 1.

Seniors living in private, non-farm households in 1991 in British Columbia were much more likely than non-seniors to live in their own home mortgage-free. Indeed, 60% of households in which the person primarily responsible for shelter costs was 65 to 74 years of age and 54% of households in which the person primarily responsible for shelter costs was 75 or more years of age lived in their own mortgage-free homes (Statistics Canada, 1993a). In comparison, among private householders of all ages in British Columbia in 1991, only 30% lived in their own homes mortgage-free.

Private householders can be either home owners or renters. In British Columbia in 1991, 30% of persons aged 65 to 74 and 42% of persons 75 or more years of age were renters. Seniors in British Columbia were more likely than seniors in Canada generally to be renters, probably as a result of heavier in-migration of seniors into British Columbia.

A great majority of seniors in British Columbia in 1991 did not participate in the labor force. Indeed, 89% of males 65 years of age and older and 95% of females 65 years of age and older were not in the labor force (Statistics Canada, 1993b). These numbers are a little higher than the Canadian average (86% of Canadian males 65 years of age and older and 94% of Canadian females 65 years of age and older were not in the labor force), indicating that seniors in British Columbia are more likely to be "retired." On the other side of the coin, these numbers indicate that in 1991 in British Columbia about 11% of males 65 years of age and older were employed in the labor force (or were looking for work) along with about 5% of females 65 years of age and older.

The median income of seniors in 1990 was higher for seniors in British Columbia than for seniors in Canada generally, higher for males than females and highest for males 65 to 69 years of age. More specifically, the median incomes of seniors in British Columbia in 1990 were $21 500 for males 65 to 69 years of age, $16 600 for males 70 and older, $11 400 for females aged 65 to 69 and $11 600 for females 70 years of age and older. Finally, the percentage of seniors with low incomes in British Columbia in 1990 was 13.8% for persons 65 to 69 years of age (compared to 15.6% of all Canadian seniors aged 65 to 69) and 20.1% for persons aged 70 and older (compared to 20.8% of all Canadian seniors aged 70 and older) (Statistics Canada, 1993c).

The median years of schooling of seniors in 1991 was higher for seniors in British Columbia than for seniors in Canada generally, higher for females than males and higher for seniors aged 65 to 74 than for seniors aged 75 and older. More specifically, the median years of schooling for seniors in British Columbia in 1991 was 11.9 years for females aged 65 to 74, 11.6 years for males 65 to 74 years of age, 10.9 years for females aged 75 and older and 10.7 years for males 75 years of age and older (Statistics Canada, 1993d). These data suggest that each subsequent generation of seniors will tend to have more years of formal education.

In summary, the youth dependency ratio is trending downward while the seniors dependency ratio is trending upward, with the result that these trends tend to be counterbalancing. The overall dependency ratio in British Columbia in 1996 is somewhat lower than the Canadian average. It appears that heavy in-migration into British Columbia has not "distorted" either the dependency ratios or the population age structure from which the ratios are calculated. Indeed, heavy in-migration has tended to offset the population aging trend.

Seniors in British Columbia tend to have a relatively positive demographic profile. Most elderly males are currently married, as are most of the younger elderly females 65 to 74 years of age. Nevertheless, the probability of being widowed increases with increasing age, especially for elderly females. Just the same, most seniors live either with their spouse or alone in private households and most of those seniors who own homes live mortgage-free. Relatively few seniors live in institutions. Nevertheless, the probabilities of living alone or of living in institutions do increase with increasing age and are higher for older females than for older males.

In comparison to other Canadians, seniors in British Columbia are more likely to be retired than are Canadian seniors generally. Furthermore, seniors in British Columbia have a higher median income and a higher median number of years of formal education than Canadian seniors generally. This relatively positive demographic profile of seniors in British Columbia may in part be a function of interprovincial and international migration patterns, which tend to select for "positive" characteristics. That is, seniors making long distance moves tend to be younger elderly who are married, able to live independently and are relatively better-off in terms of wealth and health (Northcott, 1988). The next chapter examines the health of seniors in British Columbia.

Chapter Five
The Health of Seniors in British Columbia

This chapter examines death rates for males and females of various ages in British Columbia. This chapter also compares the health status of older British Columbians with older Canadians. These comparisons use data from the National Population Health Survey of 1994-1995 and the 1991 Survey on Ageing and Independence. Finally, trends in health care utilization are reviewed.

Figure 5.1 shows the female and male death rates for 5-year age groups in British Columbia in 1994. For females, age-specific death rates for persons under the age of 60 tend to be lower than the death rate for all ages combined, which was 6.6 per 1000. After the age of 60, however, death rates rise dramatically with increasing age. The pattern is similar for males, although males at any given age tend to be more likely to die than females of the same age. There is nothing unusual about the data trends in Figure 5.1. The J-shaped curve describing the relationship between age and risk of dying has been long understood and the greater risk of male mortality in comparison to female mortality has been long identified. Furthermore, the pattern of age- and sex-specific death rates in British Columbia are similar to the pattern for all Canadians generally (data not shown).

Figure 5.1: Death Rates (per 1000) by Sex and Age Group for British Columbia, 1994

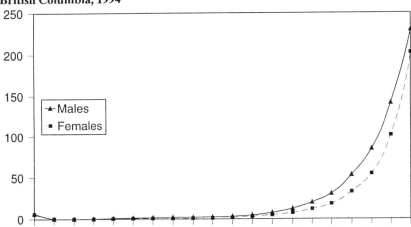

Source: StatsCan, 1996. Annual Demographic Statistics, 1995. Cat. #91-213-XPB, Table 3-13.

The National Population Health Survey (NPHS) is Canada's first longitudinal health survey. The intent of the NPHS is to interview the same people every two years asking a number of questions about a wide range of health issues. The

National Population Health Survey began data collection in 1994-95, conducted a subsequent survey in 1996-97, and future surveys are scheduled every two years following. At the time of writing, the data from the first survey conducted in 1994-95 were available for analysis.

In 1994 and 1995, the National Population Health Survey interviewed non-institutionalized persons living in every province in Canada. While some data were obtained about each member in contacted households, more extensive information was obtained from one person aged 12 or older per household. (A total of 58 439 household members of all ages were included in the survey, including 7070 members of households in British Columbia. In-depth interviews were conducted with 17 626 persons, including 2284 in British Columbia.) For this study, only respondents aged 65 and older were examined. For Canada as a whole, household members included 5302 seniors of which 3143 were interviewed in depth. For British Columbia, household members included 710 seniors, of which 421 were interviewed in depth. (In 1995, long-term residents of health care institutions such as hospitals, nursing homes and residential facilities for persons with disabilities were interviewed using a separate survey. Data were obtained for 2287 persons from 214 institutions across Canada. These data were not available for separate provinces.)

Table 5.1 shows selected health and health care variables from the 1994-95 National Population Health Survey for seniors in British Columbia, including a comparison with Canadian seniors in general. Five percent of seniors in British Columbia (compared to 6% in Canada) indicated that they had spent some time in bed during the last 14 days because of illness or injury. In total, 95% of seniors in British Columbia (and in Canada) had contacted one or more health professionals in the past 12 months. Seniors in British Columbia were more likely to have had contact with dentists, chiropractors and physiotherapists than seniors elsewhere in Canada. Some 5% of seniors in British Columbia had used alternative health care services in the past 12 months (compared to 3% of Canadian seniors). Fifteen percent of seniors in British Columbia had been a patient overnight in a hospital, nursing home or convalescent home (compared to 17% of Canadian seniors).

About 16% of seniors in British Columbia (compared to 11% of Canadian seniors) had received home care services in the past 12 months. While 69% of seniors in British Columbia (and 71% of Canadian seniors) did not need help from another person because of a health condition or problem, the remainder (about 3 in every 10 seniors) did need help with such things as heavy household chores, normal everyday housework, shopping, meal preparation or personal care.

Respondents to the survey were asked if they had any long-term conditions that had lasted or were expected to last six months or more. Seniors in both British Columbia and Canada ranked 11 conditions in the same order of frequency. Arthritis or rheumatism was the most common chronic condition, followed by high blood pressure, heart disease, cataracts, diabetes, chronic bronchitis or emphysema, cancer, glaucoma, urinary incontinence, effects of stroke, and Alzheimer's Disease or other dementia. Thirty-five percent of British

Columbia's seniors (and 39% of Canada's seniors) reported arthritis or rheumatism, while only 6 in 1000 seniors in British Columbia (compared to 7 per 1000 in Canada) reported Alzheimer's Disease or other dementia. On the positive side, almost one in every four seniors in British Columbia (23% vs. 20% of seniors across Canada) reported that they had no chronic conditions.

In summary, seniors in British Columbia appeared to be very similar to seniors in Canada generally in regard to health and health care issues. The great majority reported that they had spent no time in bed in the past two weeks because of accidents or injury. Most had not been hospitalized or institutionalized in the past year, even for one night. The great majority did not receive home care services or require assistance from another person with household chores or personal care. While the most common chronic conditions reported were arthritis/rheumatism, high blood pressure, heart disease and cataracts, in that order, almost one in every four seniors in British Columbia reported that they had no chronic health conditions. Finally, virtually none said that they were unable to get health care as needed in the past 12 months. In short, seniors generally report that they are in reasonably good health and/or that they receive needed health care services.

Table 5.1: Selected Health and Health Care Variables from the National Population Health Survey 1994-95, All Household Members Aged 65 and Older, for British Columbia and Canada

Variable	British Columbia %	Canada %
% who spent any time in bed in last 14 days because of illness or injury	5.4	6.3
% who contacted health professionals in past 12 months:		
general or family physician	87.8	86.8
eye specialist	46.3	48.8
other medical doctor	30.2	31.6
nurse	9.9	9.4
dentist or orthodontist	46.2	36.8
chiropractor	11.7	8.6
physiotherapist	13.7	7.9
social worker or counsellor	2.0	2.4
psychologist	0.6	0.6
speech, audiology or occupational therapist	2.8	3.2
any medical practitioner	94.7	94.8
alternative health care services	4.9	3.2
was patient overnight in a hospital, nursing home or convalescent home	14.7	17.0
% who received any home care services in the past 12 months	15.7	10.6

**Table 5.1: Selected Health and Health Care Variables from the National
Population Health Survey 1994-95, All Household Members Aged 65 and Older,
for British Columbia and Canada**

Variable	British Columbia %	Canada %
% needing help of another person because of any condition or health problem:		
preparing meals	6.8	7.6
shopping for groceries or other necessities	12.0	12.8
doing normal everyday housework	13.8	13.7
doing heavy household chores	28.8	26.8
personal care such as washing, dressing or eating	3.5	4.6
moving about inside the house	2.0	2.8
none of the above	68.9	70.8
% with long-term conditions that have lasted or are expected to last 6 months or more:		
arthritis or rheumatism	34.9	38.7
high blood pressure	23.6	28.6
chronic bronchitis or emphysema	6.7	5.7
diabetes	7.8	10.2
heart disease	16.5	16.8
cancer	6.5	5.4
effects of stroke	3.7	3.6
urinary incontinence	3.8	3.8
Alzheimer's disease or other dementia	0.6	0.7
cataracts	13.3	14.1
glaucoma	5.0	4.5
none	23.4	20.0
% who did not get needed health care or advice during the past 12 months	1.8	3.7
(n)	(706-710)	(5286-5302)

Table 5.2 shows additional health status variables from the 1994-95 National Population Health Survey for seniors in British Columbia, including a comparison with Canadian seniors. While British Columbia seniors often reported somewhat better health than seniors generally, there were no striking differences between seniors in British Columbia and Canadian seniors generally.

The majority of seniors in British Columbia said that their health was either good or very good, while few said that their health was poor. Few seniors indicated that they had uncorrected problems with vision or hearing. Very few reported that they had health-related speech problems. The great majority stated that they had no mobility problems and most of the remainder indicated that they were able to get around either without aids or with mechanical support. Very few reported limited dexterity as a result of problems with hands and fingers. While the majority of seniors indicated that they had no cognitive or memory problems, about 1 in every 4 seniors said that they were "somewhat forgetful." Less that 10% said that they had "some difficulty thinking," while a few reported that they were very forgetful and unable to remember things.

The majority of seniors in British Columbia reported no pain or discomfort, while few reported severe pain or discomfort. Similarly, few seniors reported having pain that prevented them from engaging in most activities. The great majority of seniors had taken at least one prescription or over-the-counter medication in the past month. Of those seniors who had taken medication in the past month, a substantial majority had taken two or fewer different medications in the past two days. The great majority of seniors said that they were happy and interested in life and most of the remainder stated that they were "somewhat happy." With respect to mental distress rated on a scale from 0 to 24, a substantial number of seniors reported no distress (scale value 0) and most seniors had a mental distress score of 3 or less, while very few had a score of 10 or more.

Seniors in British Columbia generally reported high levels of social support. In particular, the vast majority of seniors indicated that they had someone they can really count on to help out in a crisis and that they had someone who makes them feel loved and cared for. Furthermore, the great majority of seniors said that they had someone they can really count on to give them advice when they are making important decisions and that they had someone to confide in or talk to about their private feelings or concerns.

Table 5.2: Selected Health Status Variables from the National Population Health Survey 1994-95, Selected Household Member Aged 65 and Older, for British Columbia and Canada

Variable	British Columbia	Canada
	%	%
Health in General		
In general, would you say your health is:		
excellent?	13.6	12.5
very good?	31.9	27.2
good?	34.6	33.7
fair?	16.3	20.5
poor?	3.6	6.1
	100.0	100.0
Vision		
no visual problems	14.2	14.1
problems corrected by lenses	80.7	78.3
problem seeing far/not corrected	1.8	3.2
problem seeing near/not corrected	1.4	1.9
problem seeing near and far/no sight	1.9	2.5
	100.0	100.0

Table 5.2: Selected Health Status Variables from the National Population Health Survey 1994-95, Selected Household Member Aged 65 and Older, for British Columbia and Canada

Variable	British Columbia	Canada
	%	%
Hearing		
no hearing problems	81.0	82.6
hearing problems/corrected	13.5	11.4
hearing problems/not corrected	5.5	6.1
	100.0	100.1
Speech		
no speech problems	98.6	97.9
partially/not understood	1.4	2.1
	100.0	100.0
Getting Around (Mobility)		
no mobility problems	85.1	86.3
mobility problems/no aids needed	2.2	2.1
mobility problems/mechanical support needed	9.8	7.6
mobility problems/cannot walk	2.8	3.9
	99.9	99.9
Hands and Fingers (Dexterity)		
no dexterity problems	97.6	97.2
dexterity problems/no help needed	0.9	1.6
dexterity problems/need help	1.5	1.2
	100.0	100.0
Memory and Thinking (Cognition)		
no cognitive problems	59.8	62.6
no memory problems	1.4	3.9
somewhat forgetful	28.4	21.5
some difficulty thinking	7.8	8.5
very forgetful/unable to remember	2.5	3.5
	99.9	100.0
Pain and Discomfort		
Severity		
no pain/discomfort	76.9	68.7
mild pain/discomfort	5.9	9.2
moderate pain/discomfort	12.2	16.4
severe pain/discomfort	5.0	5.6
	100.0	99.9
Interferes with Activities		
no pain or discomfort	76.9	68.7
pain does not prevent activity	3.9	7.3
pain prevents a few activities	6.5	11.7
pain prevents some activities	6.6	6.0
pain prevents most activities	6.0	6.3
	99.9	100.0

Table 5.2: Selected Health Status Variables from the National Population Health Survey 1994-95, Selected Household Member Aged 65 and Older, for British Columbia and Canada

Variable	British Columbia %	Canada %
Drug Use (in past month)		
Regarding your use of medications, both prescription and over-the-counter as well as other health products, in the last month did you take any medication?		
no medication	17.0	12.9
one or more medications	83.0	87.1
	100.0	100.0
[If you took one or more medications in past month] Referring to yesterday and the day before yesterday: During those two days, how many different medications did you take?		
0	17.3	14.0
1	26.4	26.2
2	27.7	24.1
3	12.1	13.9
4	9.0	9.2
5	2.7	5.7
6 or more	4.7	6.8
	99.9	99.9
Feelings (Emotion)		
Would you describe yourself as being usually:		
happy and interested in life?	79.5	74.6
somewhat happy?	17.2	21.4
somewhat unhappy?	2.5	3.1
unhappy with little interest in life?	0.7	0.7
so unhappy that life is not worthwhile?	0.2	0.3
	100.1	100.1
Mental Health (Distress)		
(scale values 0 to 24 where 0=no distress & 24=high distress)		
0	39.9	31.0
1	18.7	17.0
2	12.9	13.7
3	11.0	10.0
4	4.5	7.0
5	3.1	5.2
6	2.1	4.5
7	1.8	3.4
8	1.4	1.8
9	1.6	1.3
10 or more	3.0	5.1
	100.0	100.0

Table 5.2: Selected Health Status Variables from the National Population Health Survey 1994-95, Selected Household Member Aged 65 and Older, for British Columbia and Canada

Variable	British Columbia %	Canada %
Social Support		
Do you have someone you can confide in, or talk to about your private feelings or concerns?		
Yes	83.7	82.9
No	16.3	17.1
	100.0	100.0
Do you have someone you can really count on to help you out in a crisis situation?		
Yes	97.0	94.8
No	3.0	5.2
	100.0	100.0
Do you have someone you can really count on to give you advice when you are making important personal decisions?		
Yes	87.4	89.2
No	12.6	10.8
	100.0	100.0
Do you have someone who makes you feel loved and cared for?		
Yes	94.5	96.6
No	5.5	3.4
	100.0	100.0
(n)	(347-421)	(2695-3143)

The Survey on Ageing and Independence was conducted in 1991. For this national survey, some 20 000 non-institutionalized persons 45 years of age and older were interviewed. A total of 7300 seniors across Canada participated in the survey, including 990 seniors resident in British Columbia. Table 5.3 compares the health and well-being of respondents 65 years of age and older in British Columbia and across Canada.

The majority of seniors in British Columbia and in Canada as a whole said that their health was good or excellent, while a minority said it was fair or poor. Seniors in British Columbia were somewhat more likely to report better health than seniors generally. Similarly, when asked to compare their health to other persons their age, seniors in British Columbia were more likely to say that their health was better and less likely to say it was worse than were seniors across Canada. The great majority of seniors said that their health was either better or about the same as other persons their age. In other words, the average person said that their health was better than average!

While about one-third of seniors said that they were limited to some degree in the kind or amount of activity they can do because of an illness, physical condition or health problem lasting six months or more, the great majority of seniors said that they were coping well with their limitations. Seniors in British Columbia were more likely than seniors elsewhere in Canada to say that they were coping well with their limitations.

Few seniors described their life as "very stressful." Furthermore, seniors in British Columbia were more likely than seniors elsewhere in Canada to describe their life as "not at all stressful." In addition, the substantial majority of seniors in British Columbia and in Canada generally indicated that in the past few weeks they had not felt lonely, depressed or bored. Furthermore, a substantial majority reported that in the past few weeks they had often or sometimes felt "on top of the world" and that "things were going their way." When seniors were asked how they felt about their life as a whole, almost all said that they were satisfied.

Almost all seniors (about 95%) in British Columbia and in Canada generally reported that they felt safe and secure in their houses and apartments. While seniors were more likely to be fearful in their neighborhoods outside of their homes, nevertheless, almost 90% of seniors said that they felt safe and secure outside in their neighborhood. For the minority of seniors who did not feel safe and secure outside in their neighborhood, most (around 70%) indicated that they limited their activities outside their homes because of their concerns. Finally, with regard to accidental injuries received at home or away from home, few seniors reported being injured accidentally in the past 12 months.

Seniors were asked if they had moved from one residence to another in the past five years. Those who had moved were then asked their reasons for moving. (Recall that the Survey on Ageing and Independence excluded institutionalized seniors and so moves into institutions are excluded from these data.) Seniors in British Columbia were more likely to have moved (27% versus 20%) than Canadian seniors generally. The single most common reason given for moving was to obtain a home of more suitable size. Other reasons given for moving included retirement, decline in health of self or spouse or death of spouse, financial reasons, desire for better access to recreation, and to receive care from a relative or to provide care to a relative.

Table 5.3: Selected Health and Well-Being Variables from the Survey on Ageing and Independence 1991, Respondents Aged 65 and Older, for British Columbia and Canada

Variable	British Columbia %	Canada %
How would you describe your state of health? Would you say, in general, your health is:		
excellent?	22.7	19.0
good?	47.6	45.1
fair?	23.0	27.9
poor?	6.7	8.0
	100.0	100.0
Compared to other people your age, would you say your health is:		
better?	47.4	43.5
about the same?	45.5	46.3
worse?	7.2	10.2
	100.1	100.0
Are you at all limited in the kind or amount of activity you can do because of a long-term illness, physical condition or health problem? By long-term, I mean a condition that lasted or is expected to last more than six months.		
Yes	37.7	33.4
No	62.3	66.6
	100.0	100.0
[If limited] How well do you feel you are coping with this limitation? Would you say:		
very well?	44.3	35.4
fairly well?	49.1	50.7
not very well?	4.9	10.8
not at all well?	1.7	3.1
	100.0	100.1
Would you describe your life as:		
very stressful?	6.7	9.7
not very stressful?	47.1	52.5
not at all stressful?	46.1	37.8
	99.9	100.0
Here is a list that describes some of the ways people feel at different times. During the past few weeks, how often have you felt:		
very lonely or remote from other people?		
often	4.4	5.8
sometimes	24.2	24.8
never	71.4	69.4
	100.0	100.0

Table 5.3: Selected Health and Well-Being Variables from the Survey on Ageing and Independence 1991, Respondents Aged 65 and Older, for British Columbia and Canada

Variable	British Columbia %	Canada %
depressed or very unhappy?		
often	4.1	4.3
sometimes	25.3	24.6
never	70.6	71.2
	100.0	100.1
bored?		
often	3.6	5.2
sometimes	23.1	24.7
never	73.2	70.1
	99.9	100.0
on top of the world?		
often	25.9	24.0
sometimes	47.8	48.0
never	26.3	28.0
	100.0	100.0
that things were going your way?		
often	27.4	29.7
sometimes	58.0	55.4
never	14.6	14.9
	100.0	100.0
How do you feel about your life as a whole?		
satisfied	93.1	93.9
dissatisfied	6.9	6.1
	100.0	100.0
In general, do you feel safe and secure in your house/apartment?		
Yes	94.9	95.4
No	5.1	4.6
	100.0	100.0
In general, do you feel safe and secure outside in your neighborhood?		
Yes	89.1	88.1
No	10.9	11.9
	100.0	100.0
[If no] Does this concern limit your activities outside your home?		
Yes	31.7	28.0
No	68.3	72.0
	100.0	100.0

**Table 5.3: Selected Health and Well-Being Variables from the Survey on Ageing
and Independence 1991, Respondents Aged 65 and Older,
for British Columbia and Canada**

Variable	British Columbia %	Canada %
Thinking about the past 12 months, were you injured in an accident around your home? We are looking for an injury that altered your routine for at least a day.		
Yes	6.4	5.8
No	93.6	94.2
	100.0	100.0
In the past 12 months, were you injured in an accident away from your home (excluding automobile accidents)? We are looking for an injury that altered your routine for at least a day.		
Yes	6.7	3.7
No	93.3	96.3
	100.0	100.0
% moving in the past five years, for selected reasons (multiple responses recorded):		
total	27.1	19.8
to provide care for a relative	1.1	0.6
to receive care from a relative	2.8	1.6
retirement (of self or spouse)	4.6	3.1
decline in health (of self or spouse)	4.1	3.4
death of spouse	0.8	1.2
financial reasons	3.4	2.3
home too big or too small	7.4	5.4
for more recreation	3.3	2.3
(n)*	(990)	(7300)

* Missing values vary depending on the survey question.

Robert Evans, Morris Barer and colleagues have examined health care utilization trends in British Columbia with a particular focus on the impact of the increasing proportion of seniors in the population. Barer, et al. (1989) analyzed the utilization of physician services in British Columbia from 1974-75 to 1985-86. They found that use increased by an average of 5.3% per year. General population growth accounted for an average increase of 1.8%, while changes in the age structure of the population accounted for an average increase of only 0.4%. The remainder of the increase in physician utilization was due to increases in per-capita use in all age groups (averaging 3% per year). In other words, the aging of the population itself had very little effect on the overall use of physician services. The authors concluded that physicians were treating people of all ages, and in particular older persons, more intensively. A study done in Manitoba by Black, et al., 1995 came to a similar conclusion.

Evans, et al. (1989) and Hertzman, et al. (1990) examined the use of acute care, extended care and rehabilitation hospitals in British Columbia in 1969,

1978, 1979/80 and 1985/86. Similarly, Barer, et al. (1987) studied acute and rehabilitation hospital utilization in British Columbia from 1971 to 1982/83. Finally, Anderson, et al. (1990) studied acute care hospital utilization in British Columbia in 1969, 1978, 1980/81 and 1987/88. These studies found that population aging per se is not a major influence on hospital utilization trends. Rather, there is evidence that elderly patients are being serviced more intensively in hospitals (see also Barer, Evans and Hertzman, 1995). As Evans, et al. (1989:435) state: "It is not aging per se that poses the threat; rather, it is what we are choosing (through our health care system) to do to and with our elderly." Furthermore, these authors conclude (pp. 437-438) that:

The widespread perception that hospitals are increasingly serving elderly patients is thus quite correct, although it is incorrect to attribute this change to the increasing proportion of elderly people in the general population. That proportion *is* rising, but the increase is not nearly large enough to account for the increase in the proportion of hospital patients who are elderly and, indeed, very elderly. . . . it is the increased rate of use *per capita* among the older age groups, and the corresponding decrease at younger ages, that is transforming hospitals into geriatric institutions.

In addition, these authors note (pp. 447-448) that: "Many of the very elderly patients who spend a long time in a hospital never get out alive. . . . The reallocation of patient days to the care of dying patients has therefore been almost entirely an increase in utilization by those who die at the end of long stays in extended care beds." In short, seniors are using more physician and hospital services, not so much because there are more seniors, but rather because the health care system is more intensively servicing seniors, especially those who are sick and dying.

Chapter Six
Public Policy and Programs for Seniors in British Columbia

Canadian public policy has generated a unique mixture of federal and provincial programs that developed in a piecemeal fashion in response to demographic, social and economic trends. While the British North America (BNA) Act of 1867 partitioned many responsibilities between the federal and provincial governments, personal well-being was presumed to be an individual and family concern and, failing that, to lie within the domain of charitable and religious work (Chappell, 1987). Health care was a notable exception, in that the administration of hospitals and asylums was assigned to the provinces. Since then, and particularly during the period of high economic growth following the Second World War, Canadians have witnessed the expansion of a complicated social safety net containing numerous initiatives for the benefit of seniors. This chapter reviews the evolution and current availability in British Columbia of social programs for seniors, in the areas of income security, employment and retirement, health care, housing and immigration.

Three principles underpin Canada's social programs: shared responsibility, universality[1] and less eligibility (Lalonde, 1973). The first two principles set up a tension in that, although the government recognizes the right of all citizens to a basic standard of living and to assistance when required, Canadians as a whole are charged with a personal responsibility to be both independent and interdependent. Further complications are introduced by the principle of less eligibility, limiting benefits to a level of support that is deemed to be adequate, but not high enough to discourage self-sufficiency (Hess, 1993). Consequently, and especially during economic downturns, debate ensues between those who uphold the principle of universality and those who champion directing social programs to those in need. As Gee and McDaniel (1993) observe, "the phrase, combining welfare state policies and a market economy introduces contradictions among competing values. The result is that few social programs in Canada today are truly universal."[2]

These contradictions are also evident in the criteria that govern the receipt of seniors benefits. Some programs come into effect at a certain age and tend to be universal in scope; others are based on need or merit (Gee & McDaniel, 1993). Whichever criterion is used, the Canadian ethos traditionally has favored the provision of benefits for the elderly as a reimbursement for a lifetime of hard work, thrift, good citizenship and payment of taxes.

Income Security in Retirement

Federal government retirement income benefits can be divided into four levels of benefits (Prince, 1993). These programs include:

1. payments paid directly to seniors, including Old Age Security (OAS), the Guaranteed Income Supplement (GIS) and Spousal Allowance (SPA);
2. public pension plans, to which citizens contribute during their working years: the Canadian Pension Plan (CPP) and a similar one for Quebec (QPP);
3. pension plans that are registered by the government for income tax purposes and, thus, regulated by the Pension Benefits Standards Act (Burbidge, 1996), such as private pension plans (RRSPs) and employer-sponsored pension plans (RPPs); and finally
4. tax credits and exemptions to encourage saving for retirement and to lessen the tax burden after retirement.

The first two address the need to relieve poverty in the elderly, while the third and fourth help citizens retain their standard of living following retirement. Until recently, OAS was a universal program, while GIS and SPA have always been distributed according to the principle of less eligibility. Shared responsibility is evident at levels 2, 3 and 4, although level 3 appears to be balanced more towards personal responsibility than levels 2 and 4, by giving citizens discretion to decide the degree to which they wish to participate in these pension savings programs.

Direct Payments to Seniors

Financial aid for the elderly was the first national social welfare program in Canada and remains the foundation of the federal government's financial benefits for seniors (Guest, 1985; Chappell, 1987). As early as 1906, the need for assistance for the aged poor was raised in the House of Commons. Twenty-one years elapsed before passage of the Old Age Pension Act of 1927, providing $20.00 a month to needy Canadians over 70 years of age, with equal cost-sharing between federal and provincial governments (Guest, 1985). This level of payment continued unchanged during the depression and Second World War, except that the federal government eventually assumed 75% of the cost (Chappell, 1987).

The original program had a means test, that is, only people who were defined as needing the pension received it. The means test was removed in 1951 with the Old Age Security Act,[3] making OAS a universal benefit. After 1965, the eligible age was reduced gradually over a five year period to 65 and following 1973, the pension was indexed quarterly to keep pace with inflation. Thus, by April 1998, virtually all elderly Canadians except for recent immigrants were receiving $407.15 monthly (Human Resources Development Canada, 1998),[4] totaling just under $5000 a year. While still touted to be a universal pension, since 1989 high income seniors have repaid their OAS through an income tax surcharge, commonly known as the "claw back."[5] The concept of universality was completely undermined by 1996, when Revenue Canada began deducting one-twelfth of the estimated "claw back" amount from each OAS payment, calculated from a senior's previous year's income (Health Canada, 1996).

Although poverty among Canadian seniors decreased between 1983, when the poverty rate was 31%, and 1995, it has not been eradicated. In 1995, 16.9% of seniors lived below the poverty line as defined by the National Council of Welfare (1997). Unattached seniors are particularly likely to be poor: 43% of single women and 21% of single men. The Guaranteed Income Supplement (GIS) is paid on an income-tested basis to about one-half of elderly Canadians (Gee & McDaniel, 1993). In 1998, maximum monthly benefits were $483.86 for single pensioners and those married to non-pensioners, and $315.17 for married pensioners (Human Resources Development Canada, 1998, April 9).[6] Although the GIS was originally conceptualized to provide adequately for seniors in need, the combined OAS and GIS guarantees an income of approximately $10 700 for elderly singles and $17 300 for elderly married couples (Human Resources Development Canada, 1998). This constitutes virtually the complete income of many Canadian seniors[7] and clearly does not completely alleviate poverty among the elderly in Canada (Gee & McDaniel, 1993).

Retirement is almost invariably accompanied by a significant drop in income (Marshall, 1995). Couples in which only the retired breadwinner, and not his or her spouse, received OAS used to be doubly disadvantaged. The Spouse's Allowance (SPA) was initiated to rectify this. Beginning in 1975, 60- to 64-year-old spouses[8] of pensioners became eligible to receive a fully indexed Spouse's Allowance (SPA), provided the combined family income was less than a speci-fied cut-off. In 1998, the cut-off income amount equaled $21 696 (Human Resources Development Canada, 1998). This amendment to the Old Age Secu-rity Act provided the same guaranteed income to couples with one member not quite eligible for OAS, as was available for families in which both partners were over 65. Originally, the SPA was eliminated if the OAS pensioner died. In 1979, that inequity was removed and the benefits were continued as a Widowed Spouse's Allowance, until the recipient, herself (because the spouse is usually female in this age group) qualified for OAS at 65. Further amendments in 1985 extended SPA benefits to all widows and widowers in this age group (Northcott, 1997; Prince, 1993). By 1998, widowed individuals in this age group who have a yearly income under $15 912 were eligible for a pension of up to $797.45 per month (Human Resources Development Canada, 1998).

Public Pension Plan

The Canadian Pension Plan (CPP) was created in 1966[9] to provide a pension equivalent to one quarter of a person's average career earnings or one quarter of the average industrial wage, whichever is smaller (Burbidge, 1996; National Council of Welfare, 1996). This amount was intended to augment the federal non-contributory pensions (OAS, GIS and SPA) outlined above, as well as any individual occupational pension plans, RRSPs, investments and savings, to provide a decent living standard during retirement. Compulsory contributions are made monthly by all working persons between the ages of 18 and 65 earning over $3500 per year, and are split equally between the wage earner and employer.[10] At age 65, pensions are individually calculated and pro-rated according to each individual's average career earnings, up to a maximum allowable amount.[11]

Subsequent legislation introduced limited flexibility to the plan. For example, individuals may begin receiving benefits at any time between the ages of 60 and 70, although early claims result in a permanent penalty of one half of a percent for each month below 65 years of the person's age when payments begin. Similarly, benefits are increased by percent for each month that pension payments are delayed beyond age 65. Although this change benefits many older displaced workers who use the CPP to fill an income gap before they receive OAS, it does limit their monthly benefits to 70% of what they would have received if they had let the pension mature until age 65. Persons who tap their CPP benefits at age 60 lose 30% of their monthly CPP pension for the remainder of their lives (Gee & McDaniel, 1991) but they collect benefits longer. Similarly, those who can afford to delay benefits can augment their monthly Canada pension by 30% after age 70 but they collect benefits for five years less in total. Allowances have also been made for people who spend periods out of the work force. Normally, career earnings are averaged to calculate a person's pension. Fifteen percent of a person's eligible months during which they did not work may be removed from the equation, provided that at least ten years remain.

Some changes to CPP regulations appear to address the disadvantaged position of women. Parents may drop out of the work force without penalty to care for a child younger than seven years of age. While this measure benefits women primarily, no adjustment is made to cover the reductions in wages, yearly increments and savings that are also associated with taking a leave from paid employment. Women also benefit from the introduction in 1978 of pension splitting of CPP credits at the dissolution of marriage. Nevertheless, Gee and McDaniel (1991) note that an application must be made for equal credit splitting and few avail themselves of it. Between 1978 and 1989, credit splitting occurred in only 21 000 of over half a million divorces. One explanation for this is that, at the time of the divorce negotiations, immediate benefits may seem more desirable than a delayed pension. Despite the above modifications, "inequalities associated with gender-based segregated occupational practices are perpetuated into older age" (LeBlanc & McMullin, 1997:295). The reality remains that, since CPP payments reflect a person's total contributions, those with long-term employment in stable, well-paid career occupations benefit more and those with interrupted work histories are disadvantaged (Northcott, 1997).

CPP also provides disability and widow's pensions. Prior to 65 years of age, those who can no longer work receive a disability pension. Once disabled contributors reach 65, they receive the usual retirement pension, calculated with no penalty for the years during which they were unable to work (Burbridge, 1996). Since 1992, if a contributor dies, his or her spouse will receive a pension if he or she is older than 45, has dependent children, or is disabled. After becoming 65, the widowed spouse will receive 60 percent of the deceased's pension (Burbridge, 1996).

Registered Pension Plans

As the cost of government pensions has increased, so has government support for registered pension plans, reflecting a political resurgence of the principle of shared responsibility. Although ostensibly espousing registered pension plans to be a private rather than public pension system, the government retains regulatory power, in that private pensions (RRSPs) and employer-sponsored pensions (RRPs) are subject to both federal and provincial regulations and minimum standards. Similar tax benefits are available from either savings plan. Contributions are income tax deductible and the principle and accumulated interest are taxed only when funds are withdrawn, by which time the retiree usually has a smaller income and, thus, is in a lower tax bracket. Government involvement in the private pension system is not without financial cost, however, given the large subsidies provided through income tax concessions (Gee & McDaniel, 1991) and the regressive nature of tax deferred savings plans (Gee & Gutman, 1995; Gee & McDaniel, 1991; Ragan, 1996).

Despite their attractiveness, most Canadians do not participate in the Registered Retirement Savings Plan. Only about 30 percent of Canadian families purchase RRSPs (Ragan, 1996:68) and the majority are high earners[12] who are doubly advantaged by RRSP contributions. Because the contribution limits are based on a percentage of income, they may contribute more money and avoid higher marginal income tax rates. Their advantage is clearly illustrated using 1991 figures. Contributors with incomes under $10 000 put aside an average of $1300 while those with incomes over $80 000 were able to contribute $7200, on average. Ragan (1996:75-77) clearly demonstrates the tax savings differential between high and low contributors to RRSPs. He distinguishes low-income contributors from high-income contributors at the $30 000 income level. Those with low incomes contribute an average of $3381. At an average tax rate of 17%, they save an average of $307 in income tax because of their RRSP contributions. People with high incomes are subject to a higher tax rate. By contributing an average of $3381, they avoid paying $879 in income tax on average, calculated at their average tax rate of 26%. In addition, fewer women than men contribute to RRSPs and their contributions are smaller. Figures for 1991 show that 20.3% of women and 28.1% of men made RRSP contributions (Gee & Gutman, 1995). For these reasons, Gee and McDaniel describe the RRSP as "a substantial government subsidization of the well-off segment of the population" (1991:462).

Compared to RRSPs, occupational pension plans (RRPs), many of which are public service pension plans, account for less than half as much annual saving by Canadians – 6.7 billion as opposed to 16 billion dollars (Ragan, 1986). The average employer sponsored plan covers 70% of earnings, as compared to the CPP at 25%, although only 39% of workers belong to an employer sponsored pension plan. As with RRSPs, fewer women than men[13] have private pension coverage, and their accumulated savings tend to be smaller. This can be explained by women's lower salaries, greater participation in part-time work, greater involvement in service sector jobs and in small firms which tend not to have pension plans, as well as the likelihood of extended periods out of the labor force. Current trends in labor force participation are reducing private pension coverage for men as well, given the increasing likelihood of part-time work, short term contract work and periodic unemployment, rather than a life-long career in a particular organization. In any case, savings in firm-sponsored pensions may tend to erode in value over time because, according to Gee and McDaniel (1991), only 29.9% of public sector plans and 0.4% of private sector plans are fully indexed to inflation. Dickinson (1996) cites figures from Weitz (1992), stating that one in three workers who are covered by occupational pensions contribute to a partially indexed plan, while only one in eight have fully indexed pensions. Nevertheless, many people, primarily higher income earners, rely on the private pension system for a comfortable retirement. According to Ragan, however, tax-deferred saving plans "impose greater costs on society than they confer in benefits" (1996:60). Overall, the effect of the private pension system is to redistribute income away from non-contributors and low-income contributors to high-income contributors, that is, away from those who can least afford it.

Tax Concessions

A major benefit of RRSPs and RRPs is the associated tax deferral, as noted above. Other income tax concessions that are available for seniors include non-refundable tax credits for age, pension income and disability, as well as the refundable goods and services tax credit. The maximum age credit is $3482 for individuals with incomes under $25 921. Above that income amount, the age credit is reduced on a sliding scale, with benefits being reduced by 15% of any excess over $25 921. The credit amount becomes zero at an income of $49 134 (Health Canada, 1996:94). Pension credits cover the first $1000 of pension income and the disability discount is $4233 (Health Canada, 1996:95). These tax credits reduce taxes for low income seniors; some avoid paying income tax altogether. Somewhat different from other tax credits, the goods and services tax credit is calculated from the previous year's income and then refunded quarterly during the next year to low income individuals.

Tax credits constitute a progressive tax reform, giving a proportionately larger tax break to those with lower incomes, because credit amounts are subtracted from the income tax owed, rather than from before tax income. Although the age credit and pension income credit[14] were originally conceived as tax deductions and therefore were subtracted from before-tax income, they were converted to tax credits in 1985. As a tax credit, the full amount is subtracted from the amount of income tax owed. Nevertheless, this change was progressive only up to a point. The most needy seniors, with incomes low enough that even without tax credits they pay no income tax, receive no increase to their disposable income from such tax reforms.[15]

It is worth remembering that, although tax provisions are federally legislated, in effect their costs are shared by the provinces. The federal government collects income tax revenues for both itself and the provincial governments. From the amount collected from residents of British Columbia, the British Columbia government receives 52.5 cents for each dollar that the federal government receives. Thus, the province bears about a third of the cost of tax concessions.

Consequently, in 1993/94 the age credit, pension credit and RRSP/RRP tax deferrals in total cost the Federal Government $1882 million for B.C. residents, and the B.C. government gave up $998 million in tax revenue (British Columbia Premier's Forum: New Opportunities for Working and Living, 1994). Other provincial income support programs are discussed in the next section.

Provincial Income Assistance

It would appear that B.C. looks after its seniors well. British Columbia is one of only five provinces in Canada to provide a "GIS top-up program" (Ruggeri, Howard & Bluck, 1994:144), although the benefit is less generous than that provided by the other four.[16] Low income British Columbia residents who receive the federal OAS and either the GIS or SPA qualify on an income-tested basis for the Seniors Supplement. Unattached seniors in B.C. with no income above the OAS/GIS received $49.30 per month in 1997, while couples received $120.50[17] (Office for Seniors, 1998). For needy seniors who are ineligible for OAS and GIS, income assistance is available under the Guaranteed Available Income for Need (GAIN) program, administered by the Ministry of Human Resources.[18] Low income seniors also qualify for a $50.00 provincial sales tax credit against their income tax. A number of other small, but universal, subsidies are available, such as a 25% deduction on automobile insurance,[19] as well as discounts for ferry and bus transportation, hunting and fishing licenses, and admission to museums, heritage sites and provincial camp grounds.

Is there any reason to be concerned about poverty among B.C. seniors? Knowing that British Columbia is one of the three wealthiest provinces in Canada and that seniors who migrate to B.C. tend to be relatively affluent (Hodge, 1991) might lead one to suspect not. Recall from chapter four that even though the dependency rate is higher, seniors in B.C. are likely to be less dependent. Nevertheless, in spite of an overall decline in poverty in Canada among those 65 and older, one in ten senior men and one in five senior women in British Columbia lived below the poverty line in 1995 (National Council of Welfare, 1997) and the median income for seniors was 44% below the B.C. median income (British Columbia Task Force on Issues of Concern to Seniors, 1989). For both men and women, the poverty rate among seniors in B.C. was exceeded by only two provinces: Manitoba and Quebec (National Council of Welfare, 1997).

Employment and Retirement Policies and Programs

The mainstay of employment programs in Canada is the CPP, a contributory, compulsory retirement savings plan that provides a pension. Not everyone who is of retirement age is retired, however. Individuals can elect to begin receiving their Canada Pension Plan as late as 70 years of age, an option that may be chosen by people who continue to work beyond the designated age of 65. The government of Canada continues to support people who wish to continue working after age 65 by offering them the same Employment Insurance benefits as other

Canadian workers (Office for Seniors, 1998). Thus, it would seem unproblematic for individuals to continue working if they so wish.

In reality, however, many British Columbia employers have a policy of mandatory retirement linked to their pension plans. This has been criticized as discriminatory on the basis of age and, therefore, contrary to Section 15 of the Canadian Charter of Rights and Freedoms. In addition, Section 13 of British Columbia's Human Rights Code states that age is a characteristic that may not be used to refuse either employment or the continuation of employment. Subsection 3 of the B.C. Code, however, removes this age discrimination stipulation for pension or employee insurance plans. Further, the Canadian Charter allows "discrimination" under certain circumstances. These exceptions have been challenged with varying results. In 1991, mandatory retirement at age 65 was upheld by the Supreme Court of Canada (Gee & McDaniel, 1991). While the B.C. Arbitration Board has supported policies of mandatory retirement as long as they are applied consistently and uniformly, the British Columbia Court of Appeal ruled the mandatory retirement of a U.B.C. professor as unconstitutional under the Charter (Harrison v. University of B.C., 1988; MacDonald & Currie, 1995). In current practice, people tend to retire at 65 or earlier whenever their pension benefits begin, but many are rehired subsequently on a contract or part time basis[20] (Flanagan, 1985, Marshall, 1995) or they set up small businesses of their own.

Health Care

Canada's universal health care insurance system was implemented in British Columbia[21] two years after the passage of the 1966 Medical Care Act, although it was not fully adopted by all provinces and territories until 1972. Medicare had taken almost 50 years to become a reality. As early as 1919, British Columbia proposed a provincial health insurance program, but it was never implemented (Guest, 1985). Nevertheless, debate was initiated in various parts of the country. Inequality in access to medical care became critical during the depression of the 1930s (Chappell, 1987), prompting further abortive attempts to provide health care for the needy.[22] For example, Health Insurance Acts were passed in British Columbia in 1936 and Alberta in 1937, but foundered, according to Guest (1985), amidst opposition from the medical profession. Saskatchewan became the pioneer province, successfully introducing universal hospital insurance in 1947, followed by medical care insurance in 1962 (Torrence, 1987). As medical science had advanced, better asepsis, antibiotics and laboratory tests made hospitals safer and medical care more effective, and the hospital became the primary focus of health care delivery. To meet this need, Canada embarked on an unprecedented program of hospital construction and, in 1957, enacted the Hospital Insurance and Diagnostic Services Act, ensuring free hospital care throughout the country.

Two of the conditions under which the Hospital Insurance and Diagnostic Services Act was formulated have shaped health care policy in Canada since then. The first was cost-sharing between the federal and provincial governments, initially on a 50:50 basis. The second was a set of five fundamental principles to which the provinces were required to adhere in their administration of health services, in order to receive federal funding. Bégin (1988:54) outlined the five principles as follows:

- "universality (covering 90-95% of people in a province with identical conditions for all);
- comprehensive medical services;
- accessibility (reasonable access to insured services);
- portability (between provinces, and to a certain extent, to other countries);
- non-profit public administration."

These same principles directed the implementation of the 1966 Medical Care Act, which established the Canadian system of medical care insurance. Although health care was constitutionally assigned to be a provincial responsibility, the federal government retained significant powers of regulation through its powers of taxation (Northcott, 1997).

Although trying to retain control over the quality and design of the medical care system, the federal government lost financial control because of its cost-sharing agreement with the provinces. The logical conclusion of the agreement was that health care costs escalated, given the federal promise to reimburse the provinces for half of their health care expenses – whatever they were – and the provinces, in turn, committing to the provision of comprehensive services in rural areas and state-of-the-art technology in larger centers. As Monique Bégin[23] recalled, "A new hospital here, a clinic there, a new wing of an existing institution, a new maternity ward, new laboratories – it all made for excellent local politics and good economic sense, since a province would then receive large sums of money from Ottawa" (1988: 55). Health expenditures doubled in the five years from 1971 to 1976, from $7.1 billion to $14.1 billion (Dickinson, 1994, Table 1, p. 108). At the same time, however, the government of Canada was affected financially by the oil crisis (Sutherland & Fulton, 1990). Consequently, in 1977, the Federal-Provincial Fiscal Arrangements and Established Programs Financing (EPF) Act abolished the 50:50 cost-sharing arrangement, replacing it with block-funding based on each province's population and limiting increases in federal transfer payments for social programs, including health care, to the growth rate of the gross national product (GNP) (Chappell, 1987; Taylor, 1987). Dickinson (1994) estimated the effect of the EPF adjustment as having reduced federal health care contributions from 50 to 25 percent.

Needs-tested funding for other health-related programs and services, separate from those covered by Medicare, had been provided by the 1966 Canada Assistance Plan (CAP), also originally with a 50:50 cost-sharing agreement. For example, social assistance and funding to allow needy people access to nursing homes and senior citizens homes was provided. In 1977, at the same time as the EPF Act was passed, the Extended Health Care Services Program provided an expansion of long term care funding. This program began with the federal government providing a $20 per-capita grant to the provinces for nursing homes and other residential facilities, such as group homes and home care. Subsequent annual increases for this program were tied to the inflation rate (Taylor, 1987).

Through the EPF, the federal government had granted the provinces more flexibility and autonomy in developing their health services. Limiting the yearly increases in transfer funds severely restricted their ability to add new health care services or expand old ones. The provinces scrambled to develop cheaper programs, aimed toward illness prevention, health promotion and home care, rather than the more expensive and highly technical hospital and medical care. In addition, the provinces instituted schemes to reduce health care spending through both cost recovery and cost reduction. Cost recovery methods included hospital user fees while cost reduction methods included the de-insuring of some services. Curbs to the medical fee structure led to extra-billing by physicians. The federal government defined these changes as reductions in accessibility, and responded with the Canada Health Act of 1984. This legislation reaffirmed the five principles of the Canadian health care system and expanded universality to 100% by including several groups under medicare that had previously been covered by Federal health programs, for example, the armed forces and Aboriginal Canadians. The Canada Health Act focused on the premise that a healthier population, achieved by eliminating inequalities in health status and in access to health care, would require fewer health services. By amalgamating the Medicare and hospital insurance programs, the Canada Health Act effectively banned extra-billing and user fees by threatening to reduce a province's transfer payments by the full amount of its previous year's extra-billing and user fees.

Federal funding of health care has eroded further during the 90s. From 1990 onward, the EPF transfers were frozen at the 1989/1990 level and, for the wealthy provinces of British Columbia, Alberta and Ontario, annual growth in CAP payments was limited to 5% per year (Northcott, 1997). Then, in the 1995 federal budget, the government announced plans to consolidate the EPF and CAP payments into Canada Health and Social Transfer, a single annual block transfer payment from the federal government to the provincial governments for social programming. The allocation of this omnibus grant among the various social programs was left essentially to the discretion of the provinces. While this was intended to allow the provinces the flexibility to shape social programming to address their differences in need, a direct consequence for the national health care system has been to change it from a unified national plan to ten provincial plans with similar basic standards and fundamental characteristics but regional differences (Bégin, 1988).

In British Columbia, the Medical Services Plan (MSP) offers medical coverage to all residents who have lived in the province for three months. Monthly premiums of $36 for a single person and $64 for a two person family are subsidized on an income-tested basis (Ministry of Health, 1997). MSP pays in full the fees of physicians and surgeons, as well as the cost of dental surgery that is performed in the hospital. All services in an acute care hospital, including accommodation at the level of a standard ward, are provided. Visits to chiropractors, naturopaths, podiatrists and physiotherapists are covered up to a yearly limit. MSP also pays for one examination by an optometrist every two years.

Seniors registered with MSP receive a gold CareCard that provides identification and access to a range of provincial seniors discounts (Office for Seniors, 1995). Of these, two areas of health care that are especially important for seniors are continuing care and assistance with the cost of prescription drugs (Pharmacare).

The B.C. Continuing Care System

Under funding that allowed the provinces to expand the health care system beyond acute care hospitals and physician services, British Columbia began developing what was to be an integrated and comprehensive system of long-term care and home care services for those persons, either disabled or elderly, who have a progressive and/or chronic health problem. A single point of entry into the Continuing Care Division offers assessment and placement in a continuum of residential and community-based services, funded either fully by the government or on an income-tested basis.[24] The underlying goal is to enable people to live as independently as possible. The in-home community support services include home support workers,[25] meal programs, home nursing, physiotherapy and occupational therapy, while the Residential Care Division provides family or intermediate care homes, private hospitals and extended care units with a range of levels of care. Family care homes are a type of adult foster care, giving care to a maximum of two long term clients. Other services include quick response teams, adult day centers, respite care and assessment and treatment in special hospital units for short term diagnosis and treatment.

According to Hollander & Pallan (1995), the efficiency and effectiveness of British Columbia's Continuing Care system is recognized both nationally and internationally. Given the relatively low rate of institutionalization of its population aged 65 and older, it is possible that British Columbia is achieving success in the stated goal of supporting seniors' independence. B.C.'s proportion of seniors in long term care institutions is 5.9%, equal to Ontario and Nova Scotia but lower than the average for Canada, at 6.2% (Greb, Chambers, Gafni, Goeree & LaBelle, 1994). Only Alberta has a lower institutionalization rate for seniors, at 5.8%. The proportion of seniors in Continuing Care facilities increases with age. Less than 2% of those aged 65-74 years, but 36% of people 85 and older, were in B.C. Continuing Care facilities in 1988 (British Columbia Task Force, 1989). However, the institutionalization rate also depends on the availability of long-term beds and one would need to examine the size of the waiting list and length of time before placement to determine whether or not needs are being adequately met.

Pharmacare

Seniors account for over 40% of prescription drug use in Canada (Barer, Evans & Hertzman, 1995). The burden of pharmaceutical costs for seniors was addressed by the B.C. government in 1974 with the creation of Pharmacare. As well as medications, this program covers the cost of oxygen therapy in the home. Originally conceived as a seniors program under the Guaranteed Available Income for Need (GAIN), coverage was later expanded to needy families and still later to all families. In 1995, Pharmacare was transferred to Continuing Care. Nevertheless, seniors, while comprising just 10% of those eligible, are responsible for 60% of the program's total costs (Consultants aim to reduce, 1989). In addition to removing the financial barriers for seniors taking required medications, Pharmacare attempts to monitor both the appropriateness and cost effectiveness of prescribing patterns, as well as promoting the "least cost" drug for prescriptions. Some of their decisions in this regard have been criticized by consumer groups and by the medical profession, generally with a satisfactory resolution.

Pharmacare may provide a safeguard against the danger of taking incompatible drugs. Polypharmacy, the simultaneous use of multiple medications which poses the danger of interaction effects among drugs that are incompatible, has long been recognized as a problem for seniors. It comes from a variety of sources, including seeing a number of different physicians for a number of different chronic conditions. Since 1995, Pharmacare's central computer registry, Pharmanet, provides an 18-month record of all medications taken by an individual and, hopefully, will flag to pharmacists any potentially dangerous combinations of medications.

Since its inception, Pharmacare costs have increased dramatically, from $10.5 million in 1974 (Consultants aim to reduce, 1989) to $406 million in 1995/1996 (Court rejects, 1996). In the five years before 1992, costs rose by an average of 16.4%, while the average yearly increases in the consumer price index were only 4.5% (Ministry of Health and Ministry Responsible for Seniors, 1993a:6). Not unsurprisingly, measures are being taken to control costs. In 1987, seniors began paying the pharmacist's dispensing fee up to a yearly limit, currently $200 (Chappell, Maclure, Brunt & Hopkinson, 1997). Other cost-containment strategies include both the Trial Prescription Program, whereby new prescriptions for expensive drugs are dispensed for only 10 days to save waste in the event of drug intolerance or side effects, and the Low Cost Alternative Plan, whereby less costly generic medications replace more expensive brand-name pharmaceuticals. In 1995, reference-based pricing was introduced. Here, one drug in each class of medications was chosen as the reference drug, the price of which would be covered and the difference for more expensive medications made up by the individual patient.[26] Statistically, seniors have supported this controversial policy change (Chappell, et al., 1997). Nevertheless, despite cost containment measures, Pharmacare's budget has continued to increase (Court rejects, 1996).

Housing Programs for Seniors

According to Gutman and Blackie (1986), Canada lagged behind other Western nations in developing subsidized housing programs. Although legislation was first tabled in the House of Commons in 1938 to help the provinces provide housing assistance for needy people, public housing only became available in the 50s, following the National Housing Act of 1944. The two objectives of the legislation were to assist private entrepreneurs to produce affordable housing and to provide housing assistance to those who were unable to afford housing on the private market. Seniors were a major beneficiary of these programs.

The social housing policies of the federal government are executed through the Canadian Mortgage and Housing Corporation (CMHC), either through federal funding or on a cost-shared basis with provincial housing authorities. The elderly and/or people with disabilities who spend more than 30% of their income on the cost of shelter are deemed to have a core need for housing assistance under the National Housing Act (CMHC, 1997; Murray, 1988). CMHC provides capital to municipalities, cooperatives and public and private non-profit organizations for building low-cost housing. It may also subsidize the rent paid by needy seniors to landlords, over and above 30% of the individual's income. In addition, partially or completely forgivable loans are available for residential rehabilitation through the Residential Rehabilitation Assistance Program (RRAP). This offers loans of up to $6500 for repairs to substandard housing (Murray, 1988). In B.C. in 1991, 93% of seniors lived in their own homes but only 6% received a rent subsidy. Thus, the majority would appear to be relatively independent.

A relatively new endeavor of CMHC, aimed at prolonging the independence of seniors, is supportive housing. Various styles and models of supportive housing complexes have been built (see Murray, 1988), the underlying principle being the increased ability of seniors to live in self-contained suites or condominiums with assistance from supportive services. These services may include meals, laundry, housekeeping help, recreation activities, or having someone in the complex who checks on the residents or who can be called when needed. Research conducted in B.C. found that older seniors, 75 and older, were most interested in supportive housing and that the most desired supports and services were personal alarm systems, resident managers or caretakers, and the availability of meals (Baker & Prince, 1990).

For some of those seniors who live independently, home ownership can be a financial struggle as their incomes decrease progressively with age. Sixty-eight percent of seniors in B.C. own their own homes (Seniors Advisory Council, 1993b). For those "house rich but cash poor" seniors who own their own homes and therefore may have considerable equity but little cash income, several home equity conversion options are available through the private sector, and CMHC provides information about them. These include the options of a reverse mortgage on the home, for which the senior receives monthly payments, or of selling the home and then leasing it back or, alternatively, leasing a unit in a housing project. Each of these arrangements has the effect of borrowing money from their own estate (CMHC, 1988) and thus should be seen as government sponsored but privately funded.

Affordability of housing is a major concern for both home owners and renters. In British Columbia, all seniors who are home owners may apply for deferment of the annual property taxes on their principal residence, the deferred property taxes being repaid either when the house is eventually sold or their estate is settled. For elderly renters, there is the Shelter Aid for Elderly Renters program (SAFER) program. On a sliding scale, calculated from the amounts of their monthly income and rent, seniors may be eligible to receive cash grants for rental assistance. In 1998, the maximum monthly income could not exceed $1700 for single seniors and $1900 for couples and the maximum rent eligible for consideration was $520 for single persons and $575 for couples (Ministry of Housing, Recreation and Consumer Services, 1998). SAFER ceiling rents have never been high enough to cover the average rents in Vancouver and Victoria (Doyle, 1989).

Thus, the federal and provincial governments have tried to provide help to keep seniors living independently and "aging in place" (Gutman & Blackie, 1986). Without such help, it is well recognized that when seniors on fixed incomes are suddenly presented with extra expenses, for example, a rent increase or a new roof for the house, they tend to rob their food budget. The concern is that such situations "will eventually lead to deteriorating physical and mental health and the probability of increased dependence on health and social support systems" (Senior's Advisory Council, 1993b:4). Without some form of housing program, many elderly people would be forced prematurely to enter continuing care facilities.

Immigration Policies

You may recall from chapter three that British Columbia has a high rate of international in-migration of seniors – higher than any other Canadian province – and that immigration of all ages accounts for close to half the population growth of the province. Recall also that recent immigration into B.C., particularly to the Lower Mainland, has favored people from Asian countries. Harrison (1996) explains this trend as an outcome of immigration policy and the desire on the part of the government to bolster the Canadian economy. Prior to 1978, three categories of immigrants were admitted to Canada: family members who were being reunited with (and sponsored by) previously admitted Canadians, refugees who were admitted on humanitarian grounds, and independent immigrants who met specific economic criteria whether or not they had relatives in Canada. This last group included working and retired persons. In 1978, the Immigration Act introduced the Business Immigration Program, creating a special category for business immigrants: self-employed persons and entrepreneurs who had enough personal resources to establish a business in Canada. Self-employed immigrants must support themselves; entrepreneurs must employ at least two Canadian residents. Seven years later, in 1985, a third category of business immigrant, the investor, was approved. To qualify, an investor must have a net worth of half a million dollars and be prepared to invest $250 000 in an approved Canadian business or, alternatively, $150 000 in business in a province that has attracted fewer than 3% of business immigrants.

The business program attracted numerous people from Hong Kong who feared the colony's repatriation from Britain to China in 1997. By 1989, the average net worth of investors exceeded $1.8 million, many of them originating in Hong Kong. In fact, between 1984 and 1992, 37% of all business immigrants to Canada and 48% of immigrant investors came from Hong Kong. If one adds to this the business immigration from Taiwan and South Korea during the same eight years, Asian immigrants comprised at least 55% of those who came in under the business program and 87% of the investors. Once business immigrants become established in Canada, they may sponsor other relatives under the family reunification policy, provided that they agree to provide for their family members for ten years following their arrival. If the majority of elderly Asian immigrants have come to B.C. as business or family immigrants, they are unlikely to become a drain on the Canadian economy or use many social services in the short term at the very least. It would be naïve, however, to assume that all Asian seniors are financially comfortable, given the poverty rate among seniors in B. C.

Many seniors require as much assistance as society will provide. The poorest seniors are those without private or work-related pensions, that is, those who have no income beyond that which is provided by the state. Table 6.1 reveals the limited government income received by four case study examples. An unattached senior receives just over $900 per month, while a senior couple receives almost $1607. Couples with one pensioner and a spouse who is over 60 but not yet eligible for OAS would need to get by on $1546. The poorest person in these scenarios, however, would be a 62-year-old unemployed widow with only the widowed spouse's allowance plus the GST rebate for a total monthly income of $814. When the average rental of a one bedroom apartment in Victoria, for example, exceeds $500 per month,[27] practically all of these individuals would qualify for a rental subsidy. The 62-year-old widow would receive more than $256[28] to pay the portion of her rent that is over 30% of her income, leaving her with only $570 for food and other necessities.

Table 6.1: Government Payments to Selected Seniors in British Columbia Who Have No Other Source of Income, 1998

Payments to Seniors	Senior Couple	Senior & 60-64 year old Spouse	Unattached Senior	Widow 62 years old
OAP	$ 814.30	$ 407.15	$ 407.15	
GIS	$ 630.34	$ 315.17	$ 483.86	
SPA		$ 722.32		$ 797.45
B.C. Seniors Supplement	$ 120.50	$ 60.25	$ 9.30	
GST Rebate[1]	$ 41.50	$ 41.50	$ 16.58	$ 16.58
Total	$1606.64	$1546.39	$ 916.89	$ 814.03

Sources: Human Resources Development Canada, 1998, Office for Seniors, 1998, [1]Personal communication with a representative of Revenue Canada, May 26, 1998.

Conclusions

In summary, this chapter outlines social programs available for seniors in British Columbia that apply to income security, employment and retirement, health care, housing and immigration. As Northcott (1997) observed, "contemporary Canadian society paradoxically maintains both its historical emphasis on individual self-reliance on the one hand, and, on the other hand, a more recent but strong commitment to social programs such as medicare and old age security" (p. 88). Historically, Canadian social programs were formulated according to the principle of universality but, as programs expanded and the economy did not, there was a shift away from universality to programs that were offered primarily to those with a demonstrated need.

Government policies arise and then are changed in concert with the trends and issues of the day. The next chapter examines emerging social issues that will affect seniors and influence policy as we enter the 21st century.

Notes

[1] Universal social programs provide equally for everyone in a particular social category. Thus, a universal program for seniors gives the same benefit to everyone older than a designated age – typically 65 years.

[2] Today, the major universal social programs that are available across the country are elementary and secondary education and health insurance.

[3] Amendments to the Old Age Security Act provide two income supplements, the GIS and SPA, financed with federal tax revenues. The Guaranteed Income Supplement (GIS) and Spouse's Allowance (SPA) are discussed later in this chapter.

[4] In January, 1998, the number of Canadians who received OAS was 3 619 538, for a total bill of just over $1.4 billion (Human Resources Development Canada, 1998).

[5] In 1997, tax provisions "clawed back" OAS benefits from those seniors whose income exceeded $53 215, completely eliminating the benefit for those with incomes over $85 528 (Human Resources Development Canada, 1998). Indexing of the ceiling amount occurs only in years with inflation exceeding 3%. Because government policies are aimed at reducing and hopefully eliminating inflation, projections reveal that, over time, persons with smaller income levels will be subjected to this tax surcharge (Gee, 1995; Gee & McDaniel, 1993; Gray, 1990) because of the lack of indexing in years with less than 3% inflation.

[6] In 1998, single pensioners with annual incomes less than $11 616 received GIS. Partial payments were provided up to the cut-off income levels of $15 168 for married pensioners and $28 128 for those married to non-OAS pensioners (Human Resources Development Canada, 1998).

[7] Poor unattached men 65 years of age and older had an average income of $12 184 in 1995, compared to the national average for unattached men of $23 763. Similar figures for poor unattached women 65 and older and the national average for all unattached women were $12 422 and 18 741; and for poor couples 65 and older in comparison to all couples 65 and older the figures were $17 905 and $38 861 (figures taken from Table 11, National Council of Welfare, 1997).

[8] Later, SPA benefits were extended to common-law spouses.

[9] Often, there is a lag between the passage of legislation and its implementation. The CPP became law in the House of Commons in 1965, contributions to the plan began in January of 1966 and retirement benefits were first paid out in 1967. A second example with an even longer lag is the Medical Care Act of 1966. Al-

though implementation began in 1968, it was not until 1972 that health insurance was fully adopted by all provinces and territories.

[10] Presently, employers and employees each contribute 3.2% of the employee's monthly salary. Self-employed persons must pay 6.4% (Revenue Canada, 1998).

[11] The maximum retirement CPP amount in 1998 was $744.79 (Human Resources Development Canada, 1998, Jan. 6).

[12] The Survey of Family Expenditures in 1992 discovered that the average disposable income of contributors in 1992 was $50 000 compared to $30 000 for non-contributors (Ragan, 1996:75).

[13] Gee and McDaniel (1991) report that 31% of women and 41.6% of men contribute to RRPs (Statistics Canada, 1990). This difference has narrowed but not disappeared during the 1990s.

[14] Both the age credit and pension income credit are slated for elimination with the introduction of the Seniors Benefit in 2001 (see Chapter 7).

[15] People who pay no income tax may still receive refundable tax credits, such as the goods and services tax credit. Payment is not automatic, however, and many who qualify may be unaware of the necessity of filling in an application form.

[16] For example, when Alberta was providing a maximum of $95 for singles and $190 for married couples, B.C.'s maximum was $49.30 and $120.50 ($60.25 each) respectively (Ruggeri, Howard & Bluck, 1994:142).

[17] The Seniors Supplement has not increased for some years. In January, 1992, the same amounts were provided (*Successful Senior Magazine*, 1997)

[18] Human Resources is the new name for the Ministry of Social Services. The B.C. Premier's Forum: New Opportunities for Working and Living (1994) reported that the number of seniors receiving this income assistance has declined to only 1700 in July, 1994. Many of these beneficiaries are immigrant seniors who have not yet met the 10-year residency requirement for OAS/GIC.

[19] In British Columbia, automobile insurance has been nationalized by the provincial government, under the Insurance Corporation of British Columbia.

[20] Marshall (1995) states that American studies show that 30% to 40% of people who "retire" from paid employment subsequently enter a part-time or "bridge" job, but that no equivalent data is available for Canada.

[21] British Columbia and Saskatchewan were the first two provinces to qualify for and adopt the Canadian Health Care Insurance Plan (Taylor, 1987).

[22] Voluntary health insurance schemes had developed in many areas of Canada. Unfortunately, poverty and unemployment prevented many from being able to afford the premiums (Guest, 1985).

[23] Monique Bégin was appointed the Minister of National Health and Welfare in 1977.

[24] Hollander and Pallan (1995) note that approximately three-quarters of recipients of homemaker services pay nothing because their total income is the minimum level provided by the state.

[25] Assistance with daily living may include a variety of services. Personal care includes bathing, dressing and grooming. Support with household tasks may include laundry, vacuuming and cooking.

[26] Physicians may make an application to Pharmacare for a more expensive drug for an individual patient, by submitting a "special authority" form requesting full payment for that drug.

[27] Personal communication with a representative of Brown Brothers Property Management in Victoria, June 1, 1998.

[28] 30% of her income is $244 (814 X 0.3). $500 - $244 = $256.

Chapter Seven
Emerging Issues in Public Policy for Seniors in British Columbia

The major challenge facing policy makers in both British Columbia and Canada today is how to provide the range of services required by an aging population within an economic climate of fiscal restraint. This dilemma arises from the decades of expansive social programming that began in a booming economy following the Second World War and that then continued via deficit financing and an accumulating national and provincial debt. The challenge now is to discover creative ways of expanding and changing existing seniors' programs, as well as developing new ones, while at the same time avoiding raising the public's anger over incremental taxation and the seemingly insurmountable cost of our public debt. This chapter will briefly review a number of official positions and policy documents that have shaped and will continue to shape programs for British Columbia's seniors, primarily in the areas of income security and health care. When we consider these policies in terms of the degree of burden that the services for seniors may place on the province of British Columbia, we can identify several emerging issues:

- expansion of community-based care accompanied by cutbacks in institutional care,
- emphasis that seniors be self-reliant, rather than rely on public services and programs,
- sustainability of seniors' benefits while reducing the deficit and debt,
- concern about regional inequity in the availability of seniors' programs, and
- questions of intergenerational equity and inequity.

Recent Government Policy Affecting Seniors

Both levels of government, provincial and federal, are justifiably proud of their social programs for the elderly, which serve as a marker for the collective commitment of Canadians to senior citizens. Over the past 40 years, income security programs have substantially reduced, although far from eliminated, poverty among Canada's seniors. Similarly, universal health care has contributed to the healthy aging of many citizens. The aging of the population is sometimes viewed as a triumphant outcome of the country's public income security and health care programs.

In times of economic restraint, however, demographic aging becomes reinterpreted as a problem. Fiscal responsibility demands that these same costly programs be reassessed. For the politician, this aging of the population means that more voters will be disadvantaged by any governmental attempts to limit seniors' benefits, with potential effects at the ballot box. By 2000, 20 percent of voters in British Columbia – and an even higher percentage in some ridings – will be over the age of 65 (B.C. Politics & Policy, 1989). Fiscal restraint, therefore, becomes a question of political priorities rather than economic imperatives (Townson, 1994:7-8). Governments have attempted to placate the seniors' lobby in Canada and to get seniors "on-side" in regard to service reform by establishing formal mechanisms for political consultation.

Co-opting the Seniors' Perspective

On May 1, 1980, the Government of Canada created the National Advisory Council on Aging (NACA) to advise and assist the Minister of National Health and Welfare on issues related to the aging of Canada's population and seniors' quality of life. NACA's mandate is, first, to research the needs and problems of seniors by stimulating public discussion and consulting with other groups that are involved in aging and, second, to make recommendations to the government. NACA works to avert ageism, asserting that all citizens of Canada have equal rights; that seniors' policies must reflect their individuality and cultural diversity; and that programs and services throughout the country must assure seniors' autonomy. Independence and autonomy for seniors means that they must be allowed to make their own decisions even when doing so involves risk (NACA, 1993a). Up to 18 seniors with demonstrated special ability and expertise in the concerns of aging are appointed to NACA's board. They serve for two or three year terms. Since 1980, NACA has produced position papers on a wide range of issues including elder abuse, health care, community services, consumer fraud, the aging labor force and education about seniors and for seniors (NACA, 1995a; Townson, 1994).

In B.C. the provincial government took a different approach. When its evaluation of continuing care in 1987 produced 700 public submissions, the provincial cabinet responded by appointing a Minister Responsible for Seniors[1] to coordinate a cross-government review of all public policies affecting seniors (British Columbia Task Force on Issues of Concern to Seniors, 1989). One of the new Minister's first activities was to establish a task force on aging which authored the 1989 discussion paper, *Toward a Better Age: Strategies for Improving the Lives of Senior British Columbians.* This document further developed the themes of security for seniors in the areas of income, access to health services, housing, transportation and personal security, first addressed in the review by the Continuing Care Division of the Ministry of Health. The overall goal for future programs and services was identified as helping seniors preserve their self-esteem through supporting their independence, social integration and personal growth. The suggestion was made that public programs should increase both information about, and access to, public services in order to overcome obstacles to seniors' security, such as declining health and declining financial resources, scarcity of suitable housing and scarcity of appropriate, affordable means of transportation. Moving the locus of care into the community was expected to be both more economical and more effective, as families, employers, volunteers and municipal authorities would assume more responsibility for the health, social and economic needs of aged citizens. Funding for seniors' programs was to be increased by $97 million in 1989-90 (B.C. Politics & Policy, 1989), the money to be used to extend the Shelter Aid for Elderly Renters program (SAFER) and the Home Owner's Grant to more people, to establish short stay assessment and treatment centers, to expand special transit services and to increase funding for Quick Response Teams[2] (see Seniors' Advisory Council, 1991, 1992, 1993a, 1994, 1995a).

The government of the day also established an Office for Seniors in the Ministry of Health and Ministry Responsible for Seniors and appointed a Seniors' Advisory Council. The Office for Seniors provides administrative support to both the Minister Responsible for Seniors and to the Seniors' Advisory Council. It is responsible for coordinating and producing information about seniors' policies, programs and services, while at the same time striving to overcome ageism in the attitudes and activities of people and organizations in B.C. The Seniors' Advisory Council, fashioned after the National Advisory Council on Aging (NACA), provides the link between seniors, their organizations and the B.C. government by meeting quarterly in various B.C. communities. Its 17 members are chosen to be representative of seniors' interests throughout the province. Since its inception, the Seniors' Advisory Council has established its own task forces to investigate and produce position papers on many topics, including elder abuse and neglect, housing, financial security, information as the key to seniors' independence, support for family caregivers, ethnicity, women and aging, the frail elderly and, finally, education for seniors and for their caregivers[3] (Seniors' Advisory Council, 1991, 1992, 1993a, 1994, 1995a).

As the federal and provincial governments appear to be addressing the needs of seniors separately and with considerable duplication, a joint federal/provincial initiative has been started to coordinate their efforts. The development of a *National Framework on Aging* began at a 1996 meeting of the federal, provincial (except for Quebec) and territorial Ministers who are responsible for seniors. This National Framework is a four phase project which "will facilitate the application of a 'seniors lens' to government initiatives at all levels, with a view to ensuring that the perspectives and needs of seniors are considered" (Canadian Intergovernmental Conference Secretariat, 1998:2). After developing a set of principles for policies and services through consultation with seniors across the country, in March 1998, the Ministers authorized the development of a national electronic database of programs, policies and information on seniors' income support, health, housing and other services, a database intended to facilitate evaluation and improvement of seniors' programs across the country. Nevertheless, while this is going on and despite giving the appearance of listening to seniors, the federal government seems to unilaterally be making sweeping changes to its income support programs.

Changes in Income Support for Seniors

Over the years, the Old Age Security (OAS), once a universal benefit, has become income-tested, with a gradual lowering of the income threshold and, thus, loss of the pension benefit for seniors at increasingly lower levels of income. The latest alteration in income benefits is a *Government of Canada Seniors Benefit* that is proposed to come into effect in 2001, combining the Old Age Security and Guaranteed Income Supplement into one single payment and eliminating the income tax adjustments that were formerly allowed under the Age Credit and the Pension Income Credit (Government of Canada, 1996; National Council of Welfare, 1996a). The age of eligibility will be extended downward to anyone over 60 and will be based on family rather than individual income. Both the family income threshold and the total amount of the payment will be fully indexed to inflation. In addition, the Seniors Benefit will be non-taxable. The benefit is targeted to exclude more of the relatively better-off households than before and low income seniors who presently receive the GIS may expect up to an extra $120 per year. In other words, while some seniors will benefit from the changes, many others will not. In contrast, the federal government expects to save significantly.[4]

Who stands to lose from the proposed Seniors Benefit? In Prince's (1997) estimation, those with family incomes over $45 000 will receive lower benefits. This group will likely include most two-income baby boomer couples when they reach the age of 65. Above a $52 000 income for single seniors and a $78 000 income for couples, no old age benefit will be paid. Particularly hard hit by this pension reform will be those born during the Second World War, just prior to the baby boom, who may have factored present levels of federal income support into their retirement planning and are now left with little time to boost their retirement savings plans. However, the biggest losers will likely be the provincial governments, whose tax revenues will decrease by $200 million a year because of this tax-free benefit (Prince, 1997), but whose expenses for social programs will remain.

While the announcement of the Seniors Benefit stimulated little public debate,[5] considerable controversy surrounds reform of the Canada Pension Plan (CPP). The debate has become public in part because changes to the CPP require agreement of at least two-thirds of the provinces, together representing two-thirds of Canada's population. Problems with the viability of the CPP arose because CPP was set up to be a "pay-as-you-go" insurance plan, meaning that contributions to the plan in a given year finance the benefit payments and operating expenses for that year. Nevertheless, during the early years of the plan, CPP collected more than it spent, saving the excess in an investment fund that was lent to the provinces at a modest interest rate. In 1973, the CPP began experiencing increasingly negative cash balances[6] because of the increase in benefits paid and, as a result, its investment fund is dwindling (Lam, 1993a; Lam, Prince & Cutt, 1996). The government's initial response was to propose gradually raising the contribution rates, projecting a rate of nearly 14% of income by 2035, divided equally between employees and employers (Western Report, 1996), compared to the current 1998 rate of 6.4% (3.2% from employees and

3.2% from employers). Other recommendations have been to raise the age of pension eligibility to 70, to raise the minimum contribution period above the present 10 years, and to invest the fund in the capital market for a higher rate of interest. In April, 1998, Parliament enacted *Bill C-2*, creating the Canada Pension Plan Investment Board, which will invest the reserve funds in higher paying securities. In addition, the CPP rules were changed for anyone who was not yet 65 on December 31, 1997 (Human Resources Development Canada, 1998c). Although the eligible pension age of 65 remains unchanged, contribution rates will rise rapidly to 9.9% (divided equally between employer and employee) by 2004 and then remain there. The 9.9% level is calculated to be a "steady-state rate" (p. 5) and is expected to keep the CPP solvent with no further increases. This strategy moves CPP away from "pay-as-you-go" funding and is designed to prevent contribution rates from reaching the level of 14%, that was anticipated under the "pay-as-you-go" formula.

Income security programs were not the only funding cuts imposed during the Canadian government's period of restraint policies that began in the mid-90s. Although elected on a platform of stimulating the economy through creating employment, the Liberal government later changed its deficit eliminating tactic to focus on cuts in spending, particularly social spending. Social programs in general came under the close scrutiny of the *Social Security Review,* which was announced in 1994, and further defined by the 1995 budget. Health care funding also was reduced and changed (McQuaig, 1995; Prince, 1997; Pulkingham & Ternowetsky, 1996a).

Has Health Care Become Just Another Social Program?

At its inception, the health care system enjoyed a privileged position in the Canadian welfare state, reflected in part by its status as a separate category for government funding. This special status was eroded when the federal health care grant to the provinces was combined with that for post-secondary education. In 1995, the government announced the *Canada Health and Social Transfer* (CHST), a single block of money to be allocated by the provinces as they saw fit among their various health, post-secondary education and social assistance services. In total, under the CHST, less money will be transferred. On the one hand, this places greater onus on the provinces to find creative ways for funding their various social programs. On the other hand, the Canada Health Act stipulates that the five principles of health care remain intact, allowing the federal government to retain some clout because, as long as the federal government pays some dollars to the provinces, penalties can be imposed. Nevertheless, how well health care programming will stand up against other compelling needs when money becomes tight during the next recession remains to be seen (Pulkingham & Turnowetsky, 1996a). "In theory, the CHST will allow provinces to be innovative and flexible. In practice, the availability of funds likely will determine how innovation and flexibility are defined" (Battle & Torjman, 1996:64).[7]

Canadian Health Care Policy: From Treating Disease to Promoting Health

The Canadian health care system was organized initially around a physiolog-ical model of disease and a medical system of treatment. In 1974, Health and Welfare published *A New Perspective on the Health of Canadians* (often called the *Lalonde Report*, after the then Minister of Health and Welfare) which heralded a shift in focus toward the prevention of disease and the promotion of health. This document is the first Canadian official statement on the importance of social and environmental determinants of health (Wharf Higgins, 1992). It endorsed the broad conceptualization of health described by the World Health Organization (WHO) in 1946 as being complete physical, mental and social well-being, rather than merely the absence of disease. In the Lalonde report, the pursuit of health was encouraged through making changes in a person's lifestyle in order to avoid the risk factors responsible for then common lethal illnesses, such as heart disease and cancer. Smoking, lack of exercise and high fat diets were especially highlighted as dangerous behaviours that could and should be modified. The challenge for fitness was taken up – but primarily by middle and upper-class citizens. Although the Lalonde report talked about environmental factors as well as personal factors in illness, it has been criticized for "victim-blaming," that is, for placing the primary responsibility for health upon the individual and ignoring broader societal determinants of poor health, such as poverty.

Despite such criticisms, Canada became regarded as a innovator in health care and, in 1986, hosted the first world conference on health promotion, which produced the *Ottawa Charter for Health Promotion* (World Health Organization, 1986). This document expanded the determinants of health beyond disease prevention and healthy lifestyles to include "peace, shelter, education, food, income, a stable ecosystem, social justice and equity" (Wharf Higgins, 1992; Labonte, 1993). The WHO definition of health promotion was "the process of enabling people to increase control over and improve their health" (WHO, 1986) and five strategies for the health care sector were outlined: creating supportive environments, strengthening community action, building healthy public policy, developing personal skills and reorienting health services to provide primary health care. This new notion of primary health care encompassed a social, political and educational health development process through which ordinary people, rather than health care professionals, "are encouraged to define their own needs and priorities for action, to resolve their problems by organizing them-selves and demanding access to needed resources and to struggle to overcome political and other barriers" (Registered Nurses Association of British Columbia, 1994:4). According to this perspective, health care delivery is planned at the local level around community requirements. Consequently, the services provided will be different depending on local needs.

Concurrent with the WHO conference, National Health and Welfare under Jake Epp released *Achieving Health for All: A Framework for Health Promotion* (1986), the "Epp Report," which specified health promotion strategies for

Canada. Consumer involvement was to tie together three strategies: fostering public participation, strengthening community health services and coordinating healthy public policy (Crichton, Hsu & Tsang, 1990). This involvement of the consumer and responsibility of the community were also implied by the mechanisms by which the strategies would be implemented: self-care, mutual aid or social support and healthy environments – at home, school, work or wherever citizens may be. However, the government was to be responsible for coordinating health policies and for mediating conflicting interests among different sectors. Although this report addressed the individual bias implied by Lalonde (1974) when it concluded, "we cannot invite people to assume responsibility for their health and then turn around and fault them for illnesses and disabilities which are the outcome of wider social and economic circumstances" (p. 12), it identified the aging population as a financial threat to Canada's economic future by stating, "The pressures created by an aging population and the growing incidence of disabilities in our society will take a heavy toll on our financial resources" (p. 12-13). The answer to the presumed aging crisis was stated to be health promotion, which promised to safeguard the economy against an otherwise unavoidable escalation in health care costs. Health promotion would ensure a reduction in "costs by shifting emphasis from expensive treatment to prevention and from the expensive health care delivery system to the informal support system with its focus on self-care and on family and volunteer supports" (Northcott, 1997:91). Similar statements can be discovered by reviewing key health policy directives from the British Columbia government.

British Columbia's Vision for Health Care

Dr. Richard Foulkes' report of a review of health care in British Columbia, the *Health Security Program Project* (1973), begins by observing that many of the recommendations made by a 1948 review of B.C. health services under Dr. G.R.F. Elliot were never implemented and are repeated in Foulkes' report, 25 years later. Foulkes recommended decentralizing health care delivery into a network of community health centres operated by a team of health care professionals and administered by seven regional authorities. Adhering to principles that match those of national health care, major goals of the new system were to be public participation in health planning, the integration of health care and socially supportive services, cost containment and efficiency. Despite the policy of decentralization, the Ministry of Health would continue to retain a role in coordination and centralized planning. As was true for his predecessor, few of Foulkes' recommendations were implemented. Exceptions included the setting up of a provincial ambulance service, a Health Advisory Board to solicit public input into government planning, and five community health centers, although these were less dedicated to preventive care than Foulkes had envisioned (MacKenzie, 1981). While the stated intention was to provide more personalized, effective and equitable health care, the government had "failed to encourage the changes in attitude and philosophy that must be at the root of any significant reform" (MacKenzie, 1981:40).

Moving Health Services "Closer to Home"

Years later, many of the same issues were repeated in the 1991 report of the Royal Commission on Health Care and Costs, titled *Closer to Home*. The stimulus for this study was the steadily decreasing share of the provincial health care budget covered by federal transfer payments. For British Columbia, the effects of the federal policy were highlighted in the 1990 decision to freeze per capita Established Programs Financing (EPF) payments at the 1989-90 levels and to restrict the growth in Canada Assistance Plan (CAP) payments to 5% per year for the wealthy provinces of British Columbia, Alberta and Ontario.[8] The pressure this policy produced and the urgency to begin serious planning for health care were reflected in the 1990 BC budget address:

> Despite the drastic cutbacks in federal government contributions, we will never compromise the excellence of the health care system in British Columbia. . . . Unless provincial governments can afford to pick up more and more of the cost, vital programs will wither and die. It is time to face this problem squarely. It is time to recognize that the federal government is walking away from the commitments it undertook in establishing our national social and economic programs (Couvelier, 1990:9059).

Closer to Home restated and endorsed the five principles of the *Canada Health Act*, universality, accessibility, comprehensiveness, portability and public administration.[9] In the report, Mr. Justice Seaton and his colleagues set out nine guidelines for reorganizing the health care system in B.C., at that time estimated to be costing the province in excess of $850 000 per hour (p. A-7). The guidelines are summarized below:

- Closer to Home. As much as is feasibly possible from a cost-effective and quality-of-care standpoint, medical services should be provided in, or near to, a person's place of residence.
- The Public First. Public interest is given priority over the interests of professionals and public servants.
- Outcomes. Only services that are judged to improve health outcomes should be provided.
- Community Involvement. Community-level decision-making by local people will guide health care delivery.
- Funding. Current levels of spending should be maintained.
- The Jericho Process. Integration of the health care system will be achieved by the breaking down of administrative walls between parts of the system: ministries, health care institutions and organizations, and educational institutions.
- Necessary Education. Hiring of health care providers who are over-educated beyond the level necessary for performing specific jobs will stop.
- Volunteers. Appropriate volunteer roles in the health care system should be identified and valued, and these tasks should not be performed by paid staff.

- Openness. Health care information should be readily available, except where privacy and confidentiality would be compromised.

The commission singled out numerous groups with specific health care needs for special consideration. Seniors were not among them. Instead, the report endorsed the recommendations of the recent Task Force, *Toward a Better Age* (British Columbia Task Force on Issues of Concern to Seniors, 1989), pointing out that health care for the elderly must emphasize health promotion, autonomy and a continuum of care composed of the home, the community and, where necessary, institutions.

Fourteen months later, the Government of B.C. launched its blueprint for health care reform, *New Directions for a Healthy British Columbia* (Ministry of Health and Minister Responsible for Seniors, 1993b; Registered Nurses Association of B.C., 1994). This document established priority actions for achieving the program's five major tenets: better health, greater public participation and responsibility, bringing health closer to home, respecting the care provider and effective management. Prominent within these tenets are two major convictions: to decrease the reliance upon institutional care, replacing it with health promotion programs in workplaces, schools and neighborhoods and, second, to appoint community health councils and 21 regional health boards to facilitate local control over health care.

In 1995, the newly established New Directions Development Division of the Ministry of Health and Ministry Responsible for Seniors issued a document titled *Policy Frameworks on Designated Populations*, in which the province's commitment to seniors' health was specifically addressed. The document stressed the points that seniors are a diverse group and that most seniors enjoy health. In this age group, the major health care consumers are those whose needs are illness-related but not necessarily age-related. Frailty and nearness to death are related to age only in that their likelihood increases with age. Furthermore, in addition to the complex and chronic health challenges associated with age, seniors are also at risk for less obvious health problems, brought on by social factors, such as poverty and loneliness. For this group, the goals of the health care system must include such items as encouraging independence, allowing seniors to "age-in-place" (that is, to remain in their own homes and communities) and reducing the functional barriers to service. These goals must be accomplished against a background of ensuring partnership and communication between seniors and the health care system, supporting informal caregivers, encouraging intergenerational activities and programs and addressing the problems associated with income, language, rural location and lack of information.

Widespread changes are usually met with some resistance. In a case such as this, where the intent was not simply to add-on new programs but, instead, to reduce or replace the current programs in order to shift personnel and funding to new ones, some people will be disadvantaged. The dilemmas this causes are evident in the political tug-of-war between the status quo and proposed modifications. These dilemmas were outlined at the beginning of this chapter and are discussed in the following. The first dilemma addresses the relocation of many health care services from institutions to the community.

Community Care vs. Institutional Care

Providing health care through community-based services is neither a new concept nor one that is unique to Canada. The Canadian health care system was originally concerned with the provision of medical services and hospital care. Since the late 1970s, government initiatives have enhanced the universally insured health services with means-tested services, such as home support, that are partly financed by CAP (NACA, 1995a). More recently, there has been a nation-wide trend to decentralized decision-making in health care planning and delivery, the reallocation of resources from institutions to the community, and the establishment of a coordinated continuum of health and social services. Throughout the Western world, health care is being reformed to rely less on acute care in hospitals. The expressed hope is that, wherever it is feasible, community care will be more health promoting, more effective, more efficient, more accountable and more responsive to individual needs than institutional care.

For an aging population, the intention is that community-based services will prevent or at least delay institutional care and provide a more technologically suitable level of care for the chronic disabilities of this age group. In contrast, the trend in recent years has been for seniors to occupy a disproportionate number of hospital beds. From 1969 to 1987, the hospitalization rate of seniors in B.C. increased by 14%, while that of non-seniors decreased 16% (NACA, 1995a). The increase was primarily for older seniors: women over 75 years and both sexes over 85 years of age (Hertzman, Pulcins, Barer, Evans, Anderson & Lomas, 1990). The assumption now is that few seniors require the technologically sophisticated treatment offered in acute care hospitals. In fact, many seniors fear the possibility that highly technical care may prolong life but lengthen severe debilitation or extend a painful death (NACA, 1995a).

This relationship between medical technology and the care of the elderly is a complex one. On the one hand, some of the increased use of acute care beds by seniors is due to procedures that can enhance the quality of their remaining life, e.g., cardiac surgery, joint replacement and cataract removal. On the other hand, the large ratio of seniors to non-seniors in active treatment hospitals is often blamed on the provision of overly technological and sometimes inappropriate treatment (Barer, et al., 1987; Ministry of Health & Ministry Responsible for Seniors, 1991; NACA, 1995a). However, 80% of the increase in the hospital occupancy rate for seniors occurred in extended care and rehabilitation units and only 20% was in acute care (Hertzman, et al., 1990). Almost invariably seniors in hospital were recovering from strokes and cardiac conditions, suffering from senile dementia or awaiting placement elsewhere. Further, the study concluded that only 9% of the overall increase in hospital stay, per capita, was due to population aging. Thus, rather than acute care, many elderly people require long-term institutional care, but there appears to be a shortage of long-term institutional beds.

To address this, the proposed plan is to reduce the number of acute care beds and increase the long-term hospital capacity in the hope of alleviating this backlog.[10] B.C.'s long-term care system divides care into 5 levels, the lowest level being "personal care," which primarily assists residents with bathing and meals. This first level of residential care is being phased out. Instead, minimal care patients will be maintained in the community with home support. Unfortunately, this reduction in institutionalization only accounts for a relatively small number of patients, while the majority (over 50%) of residents are in the heaviest category of long-term care (Greb, et al., 1994). An important goal is to develop multi-level long-term care institutions and housing complexes, so that individuals are not required to move away from their social connections and familiar caregivers when their condition deteriorates and requires a more complex level of care. The theme, *Closer to Home,* also applies to plans to increase the availability of long-term care facilities in non-urban communities, although the official statement that "It is better for long term care residents to live in a less than perfect facility within their own community than to be placed in a facility which meets all of the health, safety and building requirements, but is situated away from the residents' families and friends" (Ministry of Health & Ministry Responsible for Seniors, 1991:C-163) gives cause for concern.

To successfully move care into the community will require the development of new programs and the expansion of a vast variety of programs and services. Chappell (1995) discovered that care recipients, one-third of whom were too disabled to do their own housework or shopping, suffered from an average of 5.3 chronic conditions each. For these people, a wide variety of home support or day care services must be provided throughout the province.[11] When the B.C. government was investigating health care in B.C., 9% of seniors overall were using these home support services (Ministry of Health & Ministry Responsible for Seniors, 1991). As age increased, so did the proportion using home support, from 5% of those 65-74 years, to 14% of those 75-84 years, and 22% of those 85 and older. Palliative care[12] is one example of useful community support. To be effective, the community care of dying patients must encompass many services, including extensive home care and home nursing support, drug and intravenous therapy, home visits by physicians and considerable respite support for informal caregivers (p. C-175).

In general, the hope has been that community care will be both less costly and more effective. Once again, this conclusion rests partly on the use of medical technology. If technology can produce new and affordable "aids to daily living" that enhance seniors' independence or if medical science can ever prevent disabling illnesses, such as Alzheimer's or osteoporosis, the need for care will be reduced (British Columbia Task Force on Issues of Concern to Seniors, 1989). In contrast, as the level of sophistication of the treatments being administered in the home increases, so will the expense of home care. A most reasonable assumption is that the major cost reduction achieved by home care is achieved through reliance upon the unpaid help of informal caregivers.

Community Care's Reliance on Informal Caregivers

Developing and maintaining "caring partnerships" (Keating, Fast, Connidis, Penning & Keefe, 1997) among care receivers and both informal and formal caregivers is a primary goal of community care. The recipients of care, along with their informal caregivers, are to be included on an equal basis with professional caregivers in the planning and execution of community care, beginning with full participation in individualized discharge planning in the hospital. This degree of cooperation is meant to ensure client-centered care and a complimentary relationship between formal and informal care, rather than having one form of care as a substitute for the other. Critics are concerned, however, that the government's motivation is to off-load both the responsibility and expense of eldercare onto informal caregivers.

Informal caregivers are primarily women, who often carry the double burden of caregiving and working. Many may be forced to forego or curtail their employment and income in order to provide care. Many others are elderly women caring for their ill husbands. A 1991 national survey[13] reports that 12.7% of Canadians and 14.3% of British Columbians identified caregiving as one of their major activities (Chappell, 1995). A B.C. study of caregiving asserts that rather than using the term "the sandwich generation" as a descriptor of informal caregiving, a more apt metaphor is that of "serial caregiving." In this context, women spend most of their lives caring: first for their children, then for their aging parents and finally for their aged spouses (Chappell, 1995).

Informal caregivers are estimated to provide between 75 and 85% of all personal care received by seniors (Chappell, 1993; Health Canada, 1997-98). The reality is that, for whatever reason, although most caregivers are well informed regarding formal caregiving services, they tend to get along without them.[14] Services that are used tend to be those of homemakers, occupational and physiotherapists, transportation and the provision of medical equipment for home use. Consequently, the Ministry of Health and Ministry Responsible for Seniors recommends developing ways of supporting caregivers (1991:C-154), such as outreach services and flexible and individually-suitable respite, which may occur in the home, at adult day care or in a care facility, and could last for a few hours, overnight or for extended periods. To date, funding has been minimal.[15]

Seniors themselves, as volunteers, play an important part in the informal care system, particularly in self-help groups and other direct service organizations. A review of Canadian surveys suggests that between 20 and 50 percent of seniors engage in volunteer activities (Prince & Chappell, 1994). The average senior who volunteers has a higher education level, better health, a slightly higher income and is younger than non-volunteer seniors. The Government of B.C. relies upon this contribution from volunteers to provide a vital part of the health care system (Ministry of Health & Ministry Responsible for Seniors, 1991). Unfortunately, too much reliance upon volunteers can lead to uneven services. The seasonal migration of younger, healthier, more affluent seniors to warmer climates leaves a smaller group of volunteers to provide services for those older and more frail seniors who are left behind, and who may require more help in winter than at other times during the year (Joseph & Martin-Mathews, 1993).

Is Community Care Less Expensive?

While seniors prefer community care over residing in a care facility (Chappell, 1993), it still remains to be seen whether providing a full range of community services to all who require them will actually be less costly than institutional care. Population aging will likely require the expansion of both types of care and the development of multidisciplinary assessment teams to determine the best placement for each patient. It may be naive to hope that the policy of funding new community and continuing care services can be achieved from the savings realized by reducing the acute care system (Ministry of Health and Ministry Responsible for Seniors, 1991). As the population of the oldest-old increases, the prevalence of dementia and other severe disabilities increases. These require more intense levels of service and the eventual institutionalization of many. Baby-boomers had smaller families, so a larger number of seniors may not be able to rely on their children for support. From a purely economic standpoint, although most home support services are offered on a cost-shared basis, public money pays the bulk of the costs. Using the example of homemaker services, the government pays the full amount for over 75% of the recipients; those who are able to pay contribute an average of only $40 per month (Ministry of Health & Ministry Responsible for Seniors, 1991:C-155). The new proposals in the *Closer to Home* report include helping care recipients who are eligible for institutional care with the cost of their medical supplies (p. C-158), improving the wages and training of home support workers to reduce absenteeism and attrition (p. C-158) and paying a home support worker's wage to family caregivers who have had to stop working (p. C-160).

A number of indirect costs must also be factored into the government's calculation of expenses. Physicians visit their patients in long-term care facilities infrequently; informal and less-educated caregivers may arrange more trips to the doctor, thus raising the costs to Medicare.[16] Demonstration projects[17] and research into new modes of community care are also costly, as are the proposed university and college geriatric programs, the production of numerous educational and training materials (Health Canada, 1997-98), the foregone taxes from the proposed Caregiver Credit, as well as direct government funding for caregiver support groups and counseling services. Whether or not the provincial government's economic analysts correctly anticipate the full public costs of community care, they tend to ignore the private costs to caregivers and care recipients.

If seniors "age in place," the total personal cost of living for those receiving community care is likely to be higher than for residents of a care facility. People living at home have expenses for groceries, transportation, utilities and home maintenance in addition to any pro-rated fees they pay for home support and nursing services, while the rates for long-term institutional care are all-inclusive and hospital care is "free." Costs are not just financial. There will be the stress of arranging their own care. A significant minority of seniors who live alone have no informal support available (Chappell & Prince, 1994). If they can not establish a trusting relationship with an attentive case manager, these unfortunates will be left to organize their own care and may end up doing without services, unless they have the skills and knowledge to access and navigate the system – a system composed of numerous departments, administrators and professions, each with vested interests and, often, hidden agendas.

Caregivers also pay a price in financial, emotional and physical terms. While home nursing care was usually provided at no cost, a large telephone survey of B.C. caregivers found that over half of the caregivers reported paying at least part of the cost of adult day care, day hospitals, transportation, equipment and medical supplies, respite care and home delivered meals (Chappell, 1995). In addition, 30-50% of caregivers contributed to the cost of homemaker services, meal preparation, personal care, therapy and recreation for their care recipient. These respondents had been providing care to someone for between one month and 55 years, for an average of 7.8 years. These figures support Cranswick's (1997) study, which reported that 44% of caregivers were paying for extra expenses associated with caregiving, with 15% of the women and 16% of the men stating that financial compensation for unpaid work would help them to continue caregiving. The cost of caregiving is also associated with gender. Because caregivers tend to be women and caregivers have increased absenteeism and reduced productivity at work, gender inequality in wages and poverty is perpetuated. Other financial and occupational disadvantages, for example, reduced savings and retirement pensions as well as delayed or missed promotions, may persist long after caregiving has finished (Seniors Advisory Council, 1995b).

Shorter stays in acute care hospitals mean that informal caregivers are having to care for sicker individuals. Adverse effects on caregivers' emotional and physical health have been documented and there is also evidence that as the number of people receiving home support has increased, the number of hours of home support available to each recipient has decreased (Minister of Health & Minister Responsible for Seniors, 1991). The concern has been expressed that once CAP has been replaced by the CHST, there will be less money available for these community services (Battle & Torjman, 1996).

Caregiving can be both emotionally and physically stressful. Although fewer than 10% of caregivers feel very burdened or have difficulty coping (Cranswick, 1997; Chappell, 1995), two-thirds find caregiving to be stressful (Chappell, 1995). Adverse changes include altering vacation plans and social activities and being forced to relocate either themselves or their care recipient to live with or be closer to each other (Cranswick, 1997). The association between caregiving and depression is clear, with the prevalence of depression rising from 16% for caregivers of persons with mild dementia to 40% for caregivers of persons with severe dementia (Health Canada, 1997-98).[18] However, most caregivers report satisfaction from helping others and seeing the recipient happy (Chappell, 1995). Unfortunately, many if not most caregivers are over 60 years old and suffer from chronic illnesses themselves (Health Canada, 1997-98). As a result, physical or emotional collapse of caregivers is common and may result in inadequate or even abusive care (Seniors' Advisory Council, 1995b). Keating (1997) suggests that the capacity of the informal care system may have already been reached. With current societal trends including increased aging, increases in divorce rates and increasing female labor force participation associated with the reduction in fertility, the reasonable limit of the care that family and friends can be expected to provide may be exceeded by the demand to come.

Self-reliance of Seniors vs. their Reliance on Public Services

Seniors prefer to be independent and wish to live at home even when they become frail. As with other age groups, seniors' independence is closely linked to their self-esteem and quality of life. Increasingly, seniors (particularly older women) live alone; 68% of them own their own homes (NACA, 1993a). NACA estimates that half of them stay in their original homes until forced to move, while the other half move voluntarily to smaller houses requiring less upkeep. This does not necessarily mean that they are isolated – although some are. Many seniors have a broad network of friends, so that even those who lack a nuclear family may have numerous individuals to whom they feel close (Chappell & Prince, 1994).

Independence is related to health much more than age, although age does have a negative effect. Nevertheless, it would be a mistake to underestimate the strength of even the oldest-old. People who survive longest are likely to have higher levels of education and past occupational status, as well as an optimistic outlook. They have strong personalities. They are more likely to be happily married and involved in meaningful activities. All of these traits contribute to their ability to be independent. In 1986, the life expectancy for men who had survived to 75 years of age was 9 years and for women, 12 years (NACA, 1993a).

In many ways, seniors are a diverse group and may be less poverty-prone than is generally thought. Ironically, turning 65 boosts the income of many poor seniors. Their consumer needs may vary, depending upon when and where they lived their lives (Zimmer & Chappell, 1993). Burbridge (1996) notes that seniors, especially older women, are thrifty and their consumption declines with increasing age and poorer health. A significant number continue to save well into retirement, achieving a higher ratio of savings to income than younger Canadians do. For these reasons, Ruggeri et al. (1994) estimate that only 5% of seniors are struggling to get by, as compared to the usual estimate of 30%. They contend that Statistics Canada's misleading rates of poverty are derived from income alone, ignoring tax concessions and the benefits achieved by seniors from social programs. Consequently, they conclude that, despite their lower incomes, seniors are better off than most people assume because, proportionately, they have fewer expenses and more purchasing power than the average working Canadian.

Will Future Seniors be Healthier and Wealthier?

Future retirees may be more financially stable. The baby boomers are better educated and better off financially than any previous cohort (Carrière & Pelletier, 1995). As a group, they will have contributed to CPP longer and, with the higher labor force participation of women, double income couples can expect to receive higher benefits, assuming the rules are not changed in the interim. Similarly, the baby boomers have more private and occupational pensions and have done more financial planning for retirement. Accordingly, the B.C. government expects to pay the Seniors' Supplement to fewer people in the foreseeable future (British Columbia Task Force on Issues of Concern to Seniors, 1989). This favorable projection, however, depends on the interest rates of seniors' investments and the future viability of both the CPP and the OAS/GIS combination. In times of recession, when investments pay lower dividends, seniors' retirement incomes are also lower (Pulkingham & Ternowetsky, 1996b). Battle and Torjman (1996) caution against being too optimistic, given the aging of the population and the greater incidence of unemployment, part time and low paying jobs, as well as the financial effects of marriage breakdown. Without changes in eligibility, they estimate that the cost of OAS will increase, from $16 billion in 1995 to $39 billion by 2035.[19] Having greater facility with the political process may also mean that the baby boomers will demand more services than their predecessors. While individually the baby boomers are likely to enter retirement with more financial assets, collectively, they may nevertheless place a greater financial burden on society.

Obstacles to Seniors' Independence

Seniors, individually, face numerous obstacles to their independence. Gender is a major one. Being female is associated with another obstacle to independence in old age, when "income inequalities in later life tend to widen due to the long-term impact of income- and education-related differences in the ability to generate investment income" (Gee & McDaniel, 1991:467). Obstacles for both genders include the presence of multiple concurrent chronic illnesses, the lack of affordable and/or supportive housing, transportation difficulties (especially in rural and isolated communities) and cultural discrimination against those with language difficulties, poor literacy, and immigrant or aboriginal backgrounds. One study found that increasing age, low family income and unattached marital status are the best predictors of seniors' institutionalization (Carrière & Pelletier, 1995). Surprisingly, the authors also claim that higher levels of education are also associated with living in an institution. Their explanation is that those with lower incomes tend to have larger family support networks.

While the majority of disabled seniors live in the community, many do so without the assistive ADL[20] devices that could increase their functioning. Some seniors are embarrassed by the suggestion of using such devices and fear "giving in" to their disability; others are unaware of available technological assistance or how to procure it; and still others are unable to pay the associated cost. Although most ADL appliances are covered on an income-tested basis, others, for example, batteries for electric wheelchairs, are not (NACA, 1995a). Difficulties with English and literacy combined with a lack of readily available information ensure that those with the greatest need are often those least likely to obtain help.

Social isolation is a problem for many seniors, although loneliness and unhappiness is related more to the quality of their relationships than to the number of social contacts (Chappell & Prince, 1994). Older women have more friends than older men; older men are more likely to be married than older women; but, overall, women are marginally more likely to have daily contact with someone.

Finally, the problem of near-seniors being forced into retirement early due to employment restructuring is a relatively recent phenomenon with widely different effects on the well-being and independence of seniors (see Schellenberg, 1996). Some receive a generous "golden handshake," in the form of an indulgent retirement pension. These people tend to be those who least need it – men from high-income, white-collar positions who have already provided well for their retirement and who are quite likely to re-enter the workforce in another capacity. Many workers who are displaced from lower income jobs have to struggle to make ends meet, using up any savings they may have accumulated, until they begin collecting OAS and GIS benefits at age 65. Often these are the individuals who opt to start their CPP pension early at a reduced benefit level (see chapter six). They also are less likely to have occupational pensions or much in the way of retirement savings. Their CPP benefits may be lower even before they take the reduction necessary to start it early, due to shorter job tenure and multiple, lengthy periods out of the workforce.

In summary, forced retirement, social isolation, disabilities and numerous other obstacles (and often several of these in combination) work against the independence of seniors. Financial security serves to enhance other forms of independence, that is, a higher income allows better housing, more choices for transportation and increased options for recreation. In the final analysis, the relationship between seniors' reliance on public services and independence is complex. Some services are supplied through the volunteer activities of their contemporaries. Paradoxically, while reliance on public services might be interpreted as dependence, it must be recognized that many of the public services are necessary in order to enhance seniors' independence and self-worth and to limit the demand for even more services and institutional care.

Enhancing Seniors' Independence

The quality of a senior's housing is central to his or her quality of life and degree of independence. Living on a limited income means that house repairs and rent increases threaten the well-being of many seniors. New options in housing try to provide a middle ground between complete independence and "warehousing" seniors in an institution (see Baum, 1977). For example, the development of multi-level supportive housing complexes that allow individuals to transfer to another level of care without relocating is one promising option. In 1991 the Seniors' Advisory Council made housing in B.C. its number one priority. In 1993, it recommended higher rent ceilings for Shelter Aid for Elderly Renters (SAFER) benefits, the extension of SAFER benefits to those 50 years old and to those living in mobile homes and manufactured housing. The Council also recommended the production of a wide range of supportive housing throughout B.C., the renovation of current seniors' social housing to incorporate supportive features, and the development of a building code for all seniors' housing that permits safe access for mobility aids, such as scooters, wheelchairs, walkers and canes. The report ends by pleading urgently for affordable and decent housing for Native elders (Seniors' Advisory Council, 1993b).

All levels of government have responsibilities in regard to seniors' independence. According to the British Columbia Task Force on Issues of Concern to Seniors (1989), the federal government is responsible for income support and also for producing legislation to protect all citizens against crime. The provincial government is responsible for the protection of seniors against abuse, as well as many social and health policies that encourage independence. The Task Force also gives the province responsibility for encouraging seniors to arrange their own retirement planning through pensions and savings plans.[21] At the local level, police and fire protection and the planning and regulation of housing are necessary. Neither the provision nor the coordination of a comprehensive program of services to enhance seniors' independence and security will come cheaply. Seemingly, the old adage that you have to spend money in order to save money applies to the provision of services for the growing number of frail elderly people.

Sustainability of Seniors Programs vs. Deficit and Debt Reduction

In contrast, the federal government's highly visible and passionately debated social security review in 1994-95 rested upon the presumed equivalence of fiscal responsibility and reductions in social spending. Correspondingly, the British Columbia government has been committed to a zero-sum policy of reallocating funds for health care, stating that "new initiatives in one area must now be paid for by reductions – cutbacks – in others, rather than by adding more funds" (Ministry of Health & Ministry Responsible for Seniors, 1991:B-80). Outcome evaluation is the favored method by which programs are to be proven effective and worthy of continued funding (p. A-6). The challenge, however, is to develop valid definitions of the desired outcomes and reliable ways of measuring them. All desirable outcomes are not necessarily objective and readily observable by independent evaluators. Making informed choices among competing needs and the programs devised to address those needs will be problematic. An associated concern regarding government decision-making is the tendency of powerful lobby groups, corporate capital and bureaucratic agendas to influence political decisions.

Whether one agrees with the proposed remedies or not, the problem for all levels of government is being caught between the projected service requirements of an aging population and an urgent need to balance budgets. To illustrate the extent of the problem, with an accumulated debt of $550.7 billion in 1994-95, the national government was still working with a $37.9 billion budget deficit[22] (McDonald, 1997:91). The proposed transfer payment cuts will cost British

Columbia $824 million per year (Leeson, 1995:3). At the same time, Pharmacare costs are increasing and both community programs and long-term care facilities are being expanded.

Rising costs in health care have to be addressed somehow. Many other ways of controlling health care expenses have been proposed and tried: capping salaries, closing hospitals or reducing their budgets, improving administrative management to reduce inefficiency and waste, de-insuring non-essential services and paying physicians by capitation[23] or salary instead of fee-for-service. According to NACA (1995), neither method of paying doctors is preferable: fee-for-service encourages extra visits to the doctor and over-medication as a quick-fix cure, while salaries and capitation remove the incentive to provide exemplary care. NACA suggests somehow combining payment methods to meet individual needs in a cost-effective manner. Furthermore, critics claim that not all of the savings achieved in acute care are being transferred to community or home care programs (NACA, 1995a). "If medical care is cut back without an expansion of community care, seniors are left not with a new health care system, simply with a less adequate old one" (Chappell, 1993:48).

Cutting costs is one answer to a negative budget balance; increasing revenues provides an alternative. Changes to transfer payments reduce the federal regulatory powers over health care and may prompt at least some of the provinces to reintroduce user fees and extra-billing. At the federal level, higher taxation has been the usual, although unpopular, way for the government to raise needed funds. The best solution all-round will be to find ways to bolster the Canadian economy – full employment and changes in Canada's monetary policy are the most frequent suggestions (McQuaig, 1995; McDonald, 1997; Saving the Safety Net, 1995). Restructuring the pension system to increase its revenue base has begun already.

Recent changes to the contribution rates and investment strategy that are meant to turn around the CPP shortfall were noted earlier in this chapter. Raising the retirement age in keeping with increased life expectancy is another suggested remedy, although this raises the concern of increasing the unemployment rate among younger workers. Partial retirement with flextime, job sharing and part-time employment may be a better solution (McDonald, 1997). Finally, changing the CPP to a fully-funded insurance scheme, whereby each generation's contributions finance that cohort's pensions, is another suggestion. Lam (1993b) calculates that such a scheme, invested well, would provide a higher pension than presently available. The problem is that such a solution will not address the needs of the current group of seniors and near-seniors.

The most prevalent method employed by governments in Canada to address the imbalance between deficit reduction and the pressure to maintain or augment social programs has been neither cost-containment nor revenue generation. Instead, the favored strategy seems to be that of shifting responsibility downward: from the federal government to the provinces, from the provinces to municipalities and, finally, to the volunteer and informal sector. Roy Romanow, the premier of Saskatchewan, commented in a speech to the Canada Council on Social Development on May 24, 1996, that Canada's degree of decentralization exceeds that of any other country in the OECD (Organization for Economic Cooperation and Development). In his estimation, decentralization undermines government coordination among services "and the absence of truly meaningful national standards is a surefire way to dismantle the social safety net" (Romanow, 1996:27). A second direction of shifting expenses has been from the public sector to the private sector while, at the same time, the B.C. government recognizes that "'Privatization' of expenditures is not a way out of this circumstance. In the face of slow growth, transferring the costs of programs from government to private budgets does not make those programs more affordable, it just charges them to someone else" (Ministry of Health & Ministry Responsible for Seniors, 1991:A-11). There is, nonetheless, a definite tendency to shift the burden of care increasingly onto the private sector.

In summary, the viability of social programs in Canada will depend on finding suitable ways to balance income against expenditure. Policies will need to take into account the competing obligations of various levels of government to their citizens, in order to achieve solutions that are seen as fair.

Regional Equity vs. Inequity

Giving regional authorities the capacity to plan and execute health care and other social policy is an attempt to ensure that the programs and facilities provided in an area address the local needs. The corresponding down-side is that services may be unevenly distributed with duplication of some services between districts, and the complete lack of some services in others. If regional authorities use the moral principle of the greatest good for the greatest number, priority will be accorded to facilities and programs that address the needs of the majority. This may leave out programs that are vital for a few unfortunate members of the community. No region has sufficient funds to offer every possible treatment or social advantage. If scarce resources are allocated to a program that is used more by people from outside the area, the decision is unlikely to be a popular one. Without broader provincial standards, regionalization may deteriorate to a level of uneven services, inequality of access and a divergence among systems of health care and social services from one area to the next.

British Columbia intends to address this problem by assigning local planning and delivery of health care services to the regional boards but retaining Ministerial control for decisions that affect the whole health care system (Ministry of Health & Ministry Responsible for Seniors, 1991:B-7). The overall target of 2.75 acute care beds for each 1000 population everywhere in the province is intended to provide rural areas with similar access to local hospital facilities as those in metropolitan areas (p. B-100). In contrast to the population-based formula for allocating acute care beds, the Ministry plans to establish a "person-specific data base" (p. C-138) in order to allocate funding for programs according to a formula that will be weighted according to regional population characteristics.

These goals are noble. Their accomplishment remains to be seen. To even out access by giving rural and urban communities equal per capita facilities and programs will be expensive if not impossible, given the sparse population of most of the province. In the absence of unlimited carte blanche funding, decentralization is more likely to lead to a "patchwork quilt of programs" (Romanow, 1996:27). "Communities do have an integral role in ensuring social well-being. But they can only play this role when supported within a social and economic policy framework that does not undermine their economic base on the one hand, and on the other hand turn over to communities huge responsibilities for social development and support" (Bach & Rioux, 1996:324).

Intergenerational Equity vs. Inequity

While regional inequity is interpreted as an administrative problem, intergenerational inequity is usually interpreted more personally. Over the past couple of decades, the poverty rate for seniors decreased as benefits and pensions for the elderly increased. During the same period, salaries for working people flattened out (especially among men), taxation mounted and, in consequence, real income levels for wage-earners dropped (Burbridge, 1996). A primary purpose of taxation is to finance social programs which, in effect, transfers money from those who are working to those who are not and from those who are financially better off to those who are less well off. Watching their after-tax incomes diminish, public expenses for pensions and health care expand and their own expectations of ever benefiting from government pension programs lessen, most working adults, including the baby-boomers, are beginning to feel "hard-done-by." The burden imposed by a huge government debt and the foreign loans and interest paid to service that debt add to the perceptions of unfairness on the part of younger generations (Burbridge, 1996). Controversy over intergenerational equity and the responsibility of one generation for another have sparked ageist attitudes and prompted some social analysts to predict an "age-war" (Marshall, 1997) between class divisions partitioned by generational boundaries (McDaniel, 1997).

The health care services necessary for seniors are different from those required by most younger people. Health care reforms appear at first glance to address the chronic conditions of the elderly more than the acute care needs of younger people. From one vantage point, the long waiting lists for surgery and for technologically sophisticated imaging and other diagnostic assessment may unfairly disadvantage younger people (Ministry of Health and Ministry Responsible for Seniors, 1991:C-135). From their perspective, however, seniors also are concerned about possible discrimination in health care. In the allocation process for health care services, the use of outcome measures is intended to provide services that can be shown to extend life and improve its quality. This principle of utility is seen as a good thing, a worthy goal. The measurement of clinical effectiveness that is calculated by estimating the number of years that a treatment may extend life and then adjusting that number to reflect the quality of the life extended is called quality-adjusted life years (QALY). Seniors are concerned that if treatments and services provided are evaluated only by the principle of utility or by their provision of QALY at the lowest cost (NACA, 1995b), then long term care for seniors and the disabled may be limited for budgetary reasons.

Highly visible and emotionally-charged debates around limiting renal dialysis and other expensive treatments to those younger than a specified age have taken place in Great Britain, the United States and elsewhere (see Aaron & Schwartz, 1984; Callahan, 1987). Research funds tend to be more generously applied to developing better apparatus for micro-surgery, for example, than ADL appliances. Unfortunately, there are no simple answers in a very complex and interactive system. For example, any attempts to reduce the costs of caring for the elderly in the formal health care system are likely to place increased demands on the informal health care system. If past history is to be a guide, the increased burden will especially be applied to younger female caregivers.

Questions about intergenerational equity have become even more prominent in the debates over CPP and other pension reforms. At the macro-level, the provinces are now borrowing to pay the interest on the debt they have accumulated from the CPP investment fund. There are fears about their ability to pay off that debt as well (Gee & McDaniel, 1991). At the micro-level, working Canadians resent higher payroll taxes on the grounds that they are personally supporting today's pensioners and cannot foresee ever receiving as large (or maybe any) public pension benefits for themselves. Because the CPP plan only started in 1966, those seniors who are receiving full CPP pensions today did not contribute an actuarily correct amount to sustain their current level of pension[24] (National Council of Welfare, 1996b). According to Burbidge (1993) pre-retired and even younger people are starting to cut back their present consumption in order to personally save more for their future retirement needs. Thus, they are removing even more circulating money from the economy. Finally, increases in CPP contributions are probably not the final financial reform to hit the working cohort. Burbidge predicts that in order to safeguard the social safety net for needy seniors, changes will have to be made to the RRSP program, further reducing or eliminating the advantages that are still available to middle-income individuals.

The charge has recently been made that child poverty is increasing because old-age poverty is decreasing (Marshall, 1997). This reflects an oversimplified notion of exchange between various age groups, rather than identifying the contributions and demands by cohort. As people move through different ages their needs differ and, consequently, public benefits at any point in time are likely to be differentially assigned. As a cohort ages, it will pass through periods of greater and lesser need and through periods of greater and lesser taxation, which should in theory serve to even out the benefits and burdens over the long run (Marshall, 1997). For example, those who are now paying for the CPP pensions of those who have retired have already benefited as children, from their parents' indulgences and, indirectly, from the taxation paid by retirees during their working years. Those who feel disadvantaged by anticipated intergenerational inequity tend to forget that intergenerational transfers have already passed from older to younger age groups. Intergenerational transfers move benefits in both directions and the question of relative fairness is a complex one.

Two final points must be made. First, the intergenerational debate concentrates on differences between age groups, ignoring differences within age groups. Social programs provide support to the needy at every stage of life. To concentrate upon advantages and disadvantages associated with age groups ignores both the larger social bases of inequality in society and the consideration of the fair proportion of the GNP that should be devoted to the needy within each cohort. Secondly, the fact is that there are going to be more elderly Canadians in the future – both proportionately and numerically – and society is going to have to address their requirements (Townson, 1994). "One way or another we will be caring for the baby boomers in the future – either through increased taxes, by placing a greater financial burden on individuals or by imposing more stress on family systems. There is no free lunch" (Kingson, 1996:19).

In summary, recent government policy affecting the income security and health care needs of seniors has been shaped by concerns about the debt that has been accumulated by both federal and provincial governments. Income security programs increasingly have targeted needy seniors. While health care programming has stressed health promotion, health care services have concentrated on the long-term care requirements of current and future seniors. Amid concerns about regional and generational equity, policy makers are nevertheless having to give heed to increasingly large numbers of seniors.

Chapters six and seven outlined methods by which the various levels of government are addressing the needs of an aging population. With increasing numbers of seniors in the future, services are also likely to increase. Despite the fact that seniors make substantial contributions to society, some people contend that social programs for the benefit of seniors are becoming an increasingly large societal burden. However, whether or not seniors place a burden on society depends on the balance between their contribution and the benefits they receive.

Notes

[1] The position of Minister Responsible for Seniors is held jointly with that of the Minister of Health. Rather than two separate departments of government, there is only one entity: the Ministry of Health and Ministry Responsible for Seniors.

[2] Quick Response Teams organize community care on a priority basis for people who present themselves to Emergency Departments with health care problems that do not warrant admission to the hospital.

[3] Personal communication with Mark Bell in the Office for Seniors, October 1, 1996.

[4] An estimate of the national savings in the first year is $200 million. With the expected increase in the seniors population, yearly government savings could reach $2.1 billion in 2011 and $8.2 billion by 2030 (Martin, 1996; Prince, 1997).

[5] For an interesting discussion and critique of the way in which the Canadian government disguises its restraint policies in rhetoric and convinces the public to accept cuts to programs and increases to taxes, see "Social Policy by Stealth" by Gray, 1990.

[6] The increase in negative cash flows accelerated during the 1980s (see Figure 1 in Lam, Prince and Cutt, 1996) .

[7] Reacting to the fact that CHST payments to the provinces will come without restrictions as to how the provinces will allocate them, Bach & Rioux (1996) critically state, "The CHST represents the withdrawal of the federal government from the

social policy field and it's retreat to the role of a clearing house for tax dollars" (p. 323).

[8] These policies were later extended through 1994-95.

[9] See Chapter 6.

[10] In 1988, 5.9% of seniors in B.C. were in long-term institutional beds. Of the Canadian provinces, only Alberta had a lower institutionalization rate for seniors, at 5.8% (Greb, et al., 1994).

[11] Home support programs include the services of homemakers, nurses, physiotherapists and occupational therapists, and provide nursing care and rehabilitation, assessment, case-management, personal and social support, supportive housing, medical equipment and supplies, transportation services and adult day care (Seniors Advisory Council, 1995). Adult day care provides socialization, balanced meals, bathing if required, and possibly podiatry, hearing aid consultants and incontinence counseling (Ministry of Health & Ministry Responsible for Seniors, 1991:C-157).

[12] A 1986 study revealed that three-quarters of patients receiving palliative care at home died at home, while about the same proportion of those without palliative care died in the hospital (Ministry of Health & Ministry Responsible for Seniors, 1991:C-175).

[13] For a detailed summary of this national survey, see *Ageing & Independence: Overview of a National Survey,* Minister of Health & Welfare, 1993.

[14] At the time of the study, 37.1% had used no government provided services in the past six months (Chappell, 1995).

[15] Chappell (1993) observed that although informal caregivers request respite care more frequently than any other service, utilization of respite service is low. This poses two questions: whether respite care is widely available and whether that which is offered is flexible enough to be suitable for individual situations.

[16] A study of physician use among seniors compared the utilization rates in the United States and Canada. Although seniors in Canada see the doctor more frequently than do American seniors, the average expenditure per person is less. This likely reflects the lower fees paid to physicians in Canada. British Columbians receive fewer physician services than the Canadian average, especially in regard to laboratory and other diagnostic tests (Welch, Verilli, Katz & Latimer, 1996).

[17] Butselaar (1991) contains a good description of the Victoria Health Project which combines 13 different programs, including a wellness center, quick response teams and palliative care, into an integrated community service for seniors. Among the people served by this project, there was a 60% drop in acute care hospitalization and a 48% drop in the waiting list for residential care.

[18] Some degree of dementia affects 25-30% of seniors over 80 years of age and 40% of those over 90. In 1991, there were 200 000 Canadians with the diagnosis of Alzheimer's, a number that is expected to more than double by 2011 to half a million (NACA, 1993a).

[19] The 2035 figure is given in 1995 dollars, adjusted for projected inflation.

[20] ADL stands for aids to daily living.

[21] Saskatchewan has a contributory pension plan, which gives homemakers the chance to save for their retirement. In contrast, B.C. has historically been opposed to extending CPP benefits to homemakers (see Table 2 in Prince, 1993).

[22] Ottawa now has balanced the budget for 1997-98, possibly with a modest surplus, and plans a balance for the next two or three years as well.

[23] With capitation, doctors have a list of patients for whom they are responsible and for whom they are paid a set amount each year. While economists claim that this method of payment is cost-effective and deters the over-servicing of patients, critics charge that patients receive minimally adequate care.

[24] To sustain CPP pensions at today's levels, seniors would have had to contribute for 35 to 45 years. (Lam, Prince and Cutt, 1993).

Chapter Eight
Seniors in British Columbia:
Burden or Benefit?

This chapter addresses the question: Are seniors in British Columbia a burden or a benefit? This question as stated, however, is overly simplified. In order to recognize the complexity behind the question, it is better re-stated as follows: When and how much of a burden or a benefit are seniors in British Columbia and for whom are they a burden and for whom are they a benefit? Previous chapters have shown that, despite the attraction British Columbia has for older migrants, the concentration of seniors in the province is modest relative to other Canadian provinces. Nevertheless, seniors in British Columbia tend to be perceived as an increasing burden. Indeed, population aging in Canada in general tends to be viewed as problematic (Northcott, 1997 and 1994; McDaniel, 1987).

The purpose of this chapter is to examine the various ways that seniors might be seen as a burden and also to examine the various ways that seniors might be seen as a benefit. Different points of view are considered. Social change tends to produce "winners" and "losers," that is, some who are advantaged by the change and others who are disadvantaged. Those groups that might benefit from the population aging trend – the winners so to speak – as well as those groups that might be burdened or disadvantaged by the population aging trend, are identified. Given that the increasing percentage of seniors in the population will at the same time burden some and benefit others, this chapter examines the extent to which seniors are both a burden and a benefit.

A detailed numeric calculation of the costs and benefits of an aging population is beyond the scope of this chapter. This chapter does explore the various ways that seniors might constitute a burden or a benefit without imputing specific dollar values. This analysis shows that the different aspects of burden are counterbalanced by the different ways in which seniors constitute a benefit to society.

The most obvious consequence of the population aging trend is an increase in the relative size of the seniors age group, that is, proportionately more seniors and proportionately fewer non-seniors. It follows that the social costs of seniors will increase in relative terms while the social costs of non-seniors will decline. However, if the problem of population aging were simply a redistribution of social resources to match the redistribution of the population, then one would expect little fuss. The fact that considerable fuss is being made leads one to look further into the implications of population aging.

A decline in the relative number of young people in the population, for example, implies not only that young people will have less call on social resources, but also that many people who make a living or otherwise profit from serving young people will have less call on social resources. More specifically, fewer services will be required from persons working in obstetrics, pediatrics, child day care, education, family income support, family social services and policing (young people get in trouble with the law more than their grandparents). Furthermore, the "youth market" will experience declines in youth-oriented entertainment (from cartoons to compact music discs), youth-oriented consumer goods (from bicycles to Nikes) and so on.

At the same time as those persons who serve the declining proportion of youth are losing some of their market share and/or claim on social resources, those persons who serve the increasing proportion of seniors will tend to gain market share and/or claim on social resources. More specifically, more services will be required from persons working in geriatric medicine, pharmaceuticals, rehabilitation medicine, long-term care, private health care, health care insurance (to supplement medicare), old age income support, banking and other financial services, seniors housing, seniors travel and tourism, senior-oriented entertainment (from golf to opera), senior-oriented consumer goods (from canes to cadillacs) and so on.

In 1996, David Foot with Daniel Stoffman published *Boom, Bust and Echo* which became a Canadian bestseller. As the title indicates, this book is about the flow of generations through time, in particular, the aging of the baby boom of 1946 to 1966 and the subsequent baby bust and echo generations. (The baby boom came to an end as fertility levels dropped, producing the baby bust generation. The echo generation refers to the children of the boomers.) The subtitle of this book is "How to Profit from the Coming Demographic Shift." As the subtitle implies, demographic change has economic and social implications. The book's "pitch" is that people who anticipate demographic shifts and understand their implications can "profit," while those who fail to anticipate demographic shifts or do not understand their implications will lose out. As the dust jacket proclaims (see also page 2): "Demographics explain about two-thirds of everything: which products will be in demand, where job opportunities will occur, what school enrolments will be, when house values will rise or drop, what kinds of food people will buy and what kinds of cars they will drive." Foot then states that his book helps the reader to anticipate change and "to profit from the coming demographic shift."

The demographic shift examined in *Boom, Bust and Echo* is population aging and the central argument being advanced is that the aging of the population has economic implications. For example, it is noted that: "Population aging is a boon for the cosmetics business in general because, as people get older, they become susceptible to the lure of products that promise to perpetuate a youthful appearance and they are more likely to be able to afford them. Other industries are not so fortunate. The beer industry, for example . . ." (page 5).

Nevertheless, population aging as measured by the increase in the percentage of seniors in the population has been greatly exaggerated (Foot, 1996:11). The population is aging, but slowly. Canadian society will not be overwhelmed tomorrow by a grey-haired horde of seniors. Those who profit from non-seniors today will not be out of business tomorrow, just as those who profit from seniors will not become rich overnight. The demographic shift – population aging – is a long-term trend unfolding slowly over time. We have considerable time to anticipate and respond to the demographic shift. Foot argues that those who ignore this shift will eventually be left behind, while those who anticipate it can position or re-position themselves to take advantage of future developments.

Seniors in 1996 constituted 12.8% of the population of British Columbia. Over the next 20 years to 2016, this figure is projected to rise to about 16%. Twenty years is a fairly long period of time and an increase from about 13% to about 16% is substantial but hardly earth-shaking (Moore and Rosenberg, 1997:165). These numbers describe an on-going demographic shift. It would be unwise to ignore it and it would be smart to plan for it, but there seems to be little reason for the hysteria, overreaction and overheated rhetoric that the population aging trend tends to inspire.

The baby boomers of 1946 to 1966 will begin to move into their senior years starting in 2011 and will have fully passed into old age by 2031 (Foot, 1996:207). The aging of the baby boom will produce a seniors boom. This seniors boom is part of the demographic shift that Foot recommends we pay attention to in order to "profit." Nevertheless, keep in mind that this trend is a very long-term phenomenon. In short, the benefits of population aging will accrue slowly over time, just as the burdens of population aging will slowly increase.

To summarize, there appears to be a tendency to overestimate the "burden" of seniors in British Columbia. First of all, the perception that the province has a disproportionate and excessive concentration of seniors is incorrect. Second, the rate of growth in the seniors percentage of the population is such that the effects of population aging will occur only incrementally over a period of decades. In other words, population aging is not a cataclysmic event; it is a process unfolding slowly over time (Barer, et al., 1995). Third, seniors are not solely a burden; they are also a benefit. There is a tendency to focus only on the negative. The degree to which seniors are a burden is counterbalanced by the degree to which they are a benefit. The failure to take the positive into account leads to an exaggerated perception of burden.

Net burden is the difference between burden and benefit. In formulaic terms,

$$\text{net burden} = \text{burden} - \text{benefit}$$

which is to imply that the burden of an aging population is reduced by the benefits of an aging population. Note how easy it is to slip into negative characterizations. This formula conveys the message that burden is the major outcome and that burden remains even after benefits are taken into account. This may or may not be the case, but even before the data are amassed and the calculations made, this formula tends to prejudice the reader by emphasizing the negative. One might just as easily emphasize the positive benefits of population aging and define net benefit as follows:

$$\text{net benefit} = \text{benefit} - \text{burden}$$

In either case, this simple formula is not easy to operationalize, in part because the calculus depends on point of view. For example, seniors may be assessed as differentially burdensome or beneficial by federal, provincial and local governments; by taxpayers and non-taxpayers; by persons working in the private sector and persons working in the public sector; by businesses providing goods as opposed to services; by profit-driven enterprises rather than charities; by middle-aged persons, young adults and youth; and by reference to different time frames, including the present, near future and distant future. Furthermore, burden and benefit are often assessed in economic terms, although there are non-economic factors that can also be taken into account.

As mentioned, there is a tendency to assess burden and benefit in primarily economic terms. For example, governments tend to look at population aging in terms of budgetary revenues and expenditures. Given that population aging implies a decrease in the relative size of the labor force and an increase in the relative size of the retired population, governments tend to anticipate decreasing revenues and increasing expenditures. From the federal government's point of view, an aging population implies shrinking tax revenues from a decreasing labor force and increasing costs for old age income security and health care, two areas of heavy expenditure.

Nevertheless, it is important to remember that many seniors do have various sources of income and that many seniors do pay income tax. Furthermore, seniors who have accumulated savings in a registered retirement savings plan (RRSP) over the years and who begin to withdraw and spend these savings will often pay a percentage in tax. RRSPs are tax-deferred savings which means that seniors pay taxes on withdrawal rather than at the time of investment. In that sense, non-seniors who invest in RRSPs are a cost to the government in terms of reduced tax revenues, while seniors who withdraw their RRSPs are a benefit to the government, which can now assess taxes on that income. Is it not interesting that there are few complaints about the tax burden of supporting the RRSP program for non-seniors, while at the same time there are so many concerns expressed about the burden of supporting seniors! Besides income taxes, many seniors contribute to governmental revenues through the federal sales tax (GST). Low-income seniors, however, receive the GST rebate.

Note that assumptions about population aging leading to a shrinking labor force and decreasing tax revenues are not necessarily correct. Despite the population aging trend, the labor force is augmented currently by the baby boom, which will not begin to exit the labor force until 2011 and will not fully leave the labor force until 2031 (using age 65 as the age of labor force exit). Note also that the labor force has been and will continue to be augmented by the increased participation of women in the labor force. Furthermore, the size of the labor force is not the only factor determining tax revenues. Employment rates and productivity are also factors. Decreasing size may be offset by low unemployment rates and increasing productivity. In addition, growth in the economy tends to increase revenues. An aging population implies growing expenditures, but if the economy grows as fast or faster than the increase in expenditures, then social programs will continue to be affordable. Analysts typically conclude that the likely rate of growth of the economy in future decades will be sufficient to meet the rising costs of an aging population, assuming present levels of expenditure. However, expenditures may decline as various strategies are designed and implemented to reduce present levels of expenditure, for example, by reducing institutional care and emphasizing home care, and by replacing universal seniors benefits with benefits targeted only to the most needy. Growth in the economy over the long term coupled with a less expensive delivery of government-funded services to seniors will tend to make the aging of the population affordable from the federal government's point of view.

Provincial governments tend to look at seniors in much the same terms as the federal government. Given that provincial income tax is collected as a proportion of federal tax due, population aging tends to be seen as a reduction in provincial tax revenue and at the same time an increase in provincial expenditures for health care and services for seniors. Just the same, many seniors do pay income tax and seniors, of course, also pay the provincial sales tax when they make purchases. Furthermore, provincial governments will also benefit from long-term economic growth and, in addition, seem generally predisposed to shift a portion of the burden of caring for dependent seniors from government to the family and private sector, thereby reducing government expenditures.

At the local level, seniors pay property taxes (either as home owners or renters) and thereby contribute to the local tax base. Seniors may also have a multiplier effect that benefits local government revenues. That is to say, seniors are a market that consumes goods and services. Seniors create employment and the persons who "profit" from providing goods and services to seniors pay taxes and spend their after-tax income on goods and services which further stimulates the local economy.

It is usually assumed that the burden of an aging population is borne by taxpayers who are not seniors. This is not entirely true, given that many seniors do pay taxes. Nevertheless, inasmuch as the costs of an aging population are borne by non-senior taxpayers, then seniors might be seen as a burden to non-seniors. However, non-seniors may also feel that their taxes support programs for seniors that provide immediate benefits for themselves or that might benefit themselves in the future. Consider the taxpayer who has an aging and increasingly dependent parent, perhaps a parent suffering from Alzheimer's Disease. Taxes paid by this non-senior provide an immediate benefit to the non-senior in that services are available to his/her parent. Indeed, if the taxes paid purchase health care, income support and long-term care for the aging and dependent parent, then these programs reduce the personal burden for the taxpayer, both financially and emotionally. Without these services, the non-senior might have to personally shoulder the economic and non-economic costs of caring for this parent. Furthermore, taxpayers might see an aging population as beneficial in that programs for seniors might eventually benefit aging taxpayers themselves.

Employment produces taxpayers, and therefore, tax revenues. People employed in the private sector may profit from producing goods for sale to seniors and may profit from providing services to seniors. The demographics of population aging favor the seniors housing market, travel and tourism, financial services and even the funeral industry. The income earned by persons working in these businesses generates tax revenue. Tax revenue is used to employ people in the public sector to provide services to seniors, including the great assortment of persons who work in health care and long-term care, such as doctors, nurses, attendants, administrators, managers, therapists, pharmacists, researchers, home care workers and institutional staff, including persons working in housekeeping, maintenance and food services. Public dollars also build hospitals and nursing homes, benefitting private businesses and contractors from architects to electricians. And so the dollars go round and round.

Of course, some businesses in the private sector will complain that population aging hurts them more than it helps them. Businesses that target the youth market face an uphill slog given the demographic shift to an older population in which youth are less predominant. Other businesses that target the middle-aged and seniors markets will find demographic trends more favorable. Similarly, some persons who provide services in the public (i.e., government-financed) sector will complain that population aging hurts them more than it helps them, just as others will find their services in increasing demand. For example, population aging will tend to favor growth in health care more than in education.

Ironically, persons working in health care are often reported by the media as being frustrated by population aging. Given restrictive governmental budgets, persons working in seniors-oriented services tend to complain that budgets are not rising fast enough to keep up with the increased demand generated by an aging population. So is population aging a good thing or a bad thing from the point of view of those complaining? Do not be fooled by the complaining into thinking that seniors are a problem. Instead, they serve as a justification for demands for an increased share of public resources. In other words, the growing senior population often serves as a useful pawn that is manipulated in the hardball politics of competition for public dollars.

Employment opportunities, then, differ in an aging population, depending on which good or service a person, business, profession or trade offers. The seniors market, like any other market, prefers certain goods and services over others. The advantage of the seniors market is that it is a market that will grow over the long term.

Population aging is viewed differently depending on where people are in their own life course. Seniors, aware of the many contributions they have made over a lifetime and aware of the contributions that they continue to make, often wonder why they are labelled such a burden.

The middle-aged, as mentioned earlier, might complain about taxes paid to support an aging population and yet at the same time tend to think of the benefits that come to their own aging parents and that might soon come to themselves as they age in turn. Young adults might be most likely to resent the burden of an aging population. From their perspective, they will be required to pay taxes over an entire working life of some 40 years or so to support a large and growing group of seniors with no guarantee that similar benefits will be in place 40 years later when today's young adults finally reach old age themselves. Nevertheless, young people should not and probably do not focus solely on the taxpayer costs of supporting an aging population. Population aging also means long-term growth in the seniors market. As today's young people contemplate their future careers, they might consider the various employment opportunities that this growing market represents.

Burden and benefit may be assessed differently depending on one's time frame of reference. Suppose a small community in British Columbia experienced a large and sudden influx of retirees coming from other provinces. To exaggerate the point of this scenario, assume that this is a one-time influx of seniors. What would be the immediate, short term and long term consequences with respect to burden and benefit? The immediate impact of these in-migrating seniors would tend to be beneficial rather than burdensome (Deller, 1995; Chestnut, 1993; Serow and Haas, 1992; Glasgow and Reeder, 1990; Serow, 1990; Hodge, 1989). In-migrating seniors tend to be younger elderly rather than older elderly and tend to be relatively well off in terms of both finances and health. These new senior residents would purchase or rent housing, boosting the housing market and increasing the tax base. They would tend to bring their pensions and savings and utilize banking and other financial services. They would regularly patronize golf courses, stimulating that industry. They would purchase travel packages from the local travel agencies and would, in addition, attract tourism in the form of families and friends coming to visit. At the same time, they would tend to make few demands on health or social services and there is some evidence that at least some of the seniors who do become dependent would move back to the province of origin and/or move to be near family members, who could then provide assistance as needed.

Beyond the immediate benefits of an influx of seniors, the local community would continue to benefit in the short term from the presence of these seniors, who might well continue to constitute a viable seniors market/retirement industry (Zimmer and Chappell, 1993). However, as this group of seniors ages, health problems become more likely and businesses offering consumer goods and services tend to benefit less. Just the same, increasing demand for health care, home care and long-term care will benefit persons offering these services. While many of these health care services will be offered by government-funded agencies, the local community might benefit as it attracts government dollars for hospitals, nursing homes, old age homes, home care and medical care. As Foot (1996:168) says:

> Governments should view small-town hospitals not as a burden on the health care budget but as a powerful tool for the economic development of rural regions. In the years to come, the reassuring presence of a good local hospital will act as a magnet for relatively prosperous new retirees, whose arrival will create new demand for goods and services. These people will bring new wealth with them . . . It is already happening in the Okanagan and other parts of the B.C. interior, where people from Vancouver and other major cities have settled after deciding to trade their city homes for some small-town tranquillity.

Pursuing this seniors in-migration scenario into the distant future, the death rate will rise and the funeral industry will benefit. However, the demand for health care services by an increasingly dependent population might be seen increasingly as a burden, because few outside of health care would profit directly from this group of older elderly persons. On the other hand, people employed in health care will spend their dollars to the benefit of local businesses and services.

This analysis suggests that an influx of seniors is most beneficial in the immediate and short term, but becomes less beneficial and more burdensome in the long term. The contrast between short term and long term benefits and burdens would be reduced if there were a continuing in-flow of younger elderly to counterbalance the presence of older elderly.

Returning to the larger discussion of the burdens versus the benefits of population aging, seniors can also be a source of experienced and skilled but relatively cheap labor. Many retirees who neither need nor wish to work full time, are still pleased to work part time or for limited periods of time for a little extra money and/or for the pleasure of being involved and feeling that they are making a contribution to society.

As a last observation on the economic benefits of an aging population, note that charitable enterprises will tend to benefit from an aging population (Foot, 1996:210). Besides financial contributions to charities, seniors are an important source of volunteer labor. And seniors often provide benefits even in death. Bequests to universities, health research and so on may be a part of a senior's last will and testament.

Turning to the non-economic benefits and burdens of an aging population, a society composed of seniors does have a different character than a society composed of young families with a preponderance of teenagers. A society like Canada, under the influence of the baby boom, has been described as youth-oriented and indeed "in love with youth," and ageism does persist (people typically love their grandparents, but are often ambivalent and even hostile in regard to seniors generally). Nevertheless there are some advantages to population aging. Seniors are less likely to paint graffiti on public places, less likely to play their radios loudly in the park, less likely to drink irresponsibly or drive overly aggressively, less likely to mug you or break into your home in search of money to support their drug addiction, less likely to become unemployed, and less likely to get pregnant and abandon their families or become dependent on social assistance. Now the foregoing might be characterized as youth-bashing, and it is. The truth is that youth, like seniors, are both a burden in some respects and a benefit in others. My purpose is to point out, in admittedly stereotypical terms, the burden of a youthful population and therefore some of the benefits of an older population. Seniors are not kids. While the benefits of youth are not present in a community dominated by seniors, in addition, the problems that are associated with youth are also not present in a community dominated by seniors. In other words, one of the benefits of an older population is that the problems of a youthful population are largely absent.

Just the same, the problems of a youthful population tend to be overlooked or at least borne willingly. Consider the legendary baby boom, which came into being in Canada during two decades of relatively high fertility following the Second World War. The baby boom received a great deal of attention, mostly of an enthusiastic nature (Owram, 1996). Nevertheless, the baby boom meant increased demands on both families and society. The babies needed birthing rooms in hospitals, pediatric care and diapers. The children needed food, clothing, housing, parenting, education, entertainment, policing and eventually employment. These needs were met willingly and enthusiastically by parents, communities and governments. The baby boom was portrayed largely in positive terms. For the most part, the baby boomers were <u>not</u> viewed as a threat, or problem, or crisis. Children grow up and the promises of the future encouraged all to view the baby boom in positive terms.

This positive characterization of the boomers has tended to follow them into middle age. However, society has begun to show signs of a changing attitude toward boomers, who will in the second decade of the 21st century become a seniors boom, exaggerating the on-going aging trend. This latest stage of the boomer saga is anticipated in negative rather than positive terms. One might ask why the benefits of the boomer generation have been emphasized and the burdens minimized when the boomers were young, but when the boomers become old, burdens are anticipated while benefits are overlooked. It seems that there is a deeply ingrained ageism operating. Youth is good and youth is valued. Old age, on the other hand, is bad and seniors are viewed as a threat, a problem, an unwelcome challenge and a coming crisis. Perhaps this ageism comes from focusing on the future. As mentioned, youth grow up and have the promises of the future ahead of them. Seniors, however, grow older and die. Youth, vitality and life are valued while old age, frailty and death are feared. The burdens of youth seem less problematic given the promises of the future. However, the burdens of old age seem heavier given the nearness of death.

It is inconsistent and more than a little ageist to willingly shoulder the burdens of youth and then grudgingly complain about the burdens of seniors. Each generation has its burdens and benefits. We need to look more carefully and present a more balanced assessment. Canadians have been generous to the young, shouldering their burden and emphasizing the positive. Why should Canadians not also be generous to the old, shouldering their burden and emphasizing the positive? Besides, there are real benefits to an aging population, just as there are real costs. The burdens of an aging population are counterbalanced by the benefits that seniors bring. But what is the balance between the pros and the cons? Is population aging good or bad, burden or benefit? David Foot (1996:210) states: "The answer is that it is neither. It is simply a fact of life, and the better we understand it, the better we can prepare for the changes before they occur and adjust to them once they have taken place."

We have been arguing that seniors are both a burden and a benefit. However, Foot points out that our attitude toward seniors should not depend on a mercenary calculus of their relative costs and benefits. In the end, it is a simple fact that population aging is a contemporary trend and seniors are becoming an increasingly large group in Canadian society. There is no need for hysteria. However, there is a need for careful analysis, realistic understanding and a willingness to make changes. There is a need to do what must be done to provide a decent quality of life for all of society's members, young and old alike, remembering that each generation offers both burdens to be borne and benefits to be enjoyed.

References

Aaron, Henry A. and William B. Schwartz. 1984. *The Painful Prescription: Rationing Hospital Care*. Washington, DC: The Brookings Institution.

Anderson, Geoffrey M., Indra R. Pulcins, Morris L. Barer, Robert G. Evans and Clyde Hertzman. 1990. "Acute care hospital utilization under Canadian national health insurance: The British Columbia experience from 1969 to 1988." *Inquiry* 27:352-358.

Bach, Michael and Marcia Rioux. 1996. "Social policy, devolution and disability: Back to notions of the worthy poor?" In J. Pulkingham and G. Ternowetsky, (eds.), *Remaking Canadian Social Policy: Social Security in the Late 1990s*. Halifax: Fernwood Publishing.

Baker, Paul M. and Michael J. Prince. 1990. "Supportive housing preferences among the elderly." *Journal of Housing for the Elderly* 7(1):5-23.

Barer, Morris L., Robert G. Evans and Clyde Hertzman. 1995. "Avalanche or glacier?: Health care and the demographic rhetoric." *Canadian Journal on Aging* 14(2):193-224.

Barer, Morris L., Robert G. Evans, Clyde Hertzman and Jonathan Lomas. 1987. "Aging and health care utilization: New evidence on old fallacies." *Social Science & Medicine* 24(10):851-862.

Barer, Morris L., Indra R. Pulcins, Robert G. Evans, Clyde Hertzman, Jonathan Lomas and Geoffrey M. Anderson. 1989. "Trends in the use of medical services by the elderly in British Columbia." *Canadian Medical Association Journal* 141:39-45.

Battle, Ken and Sherri Torjman. 1996. "Desperately seeking substance: A commentary on the social security review." In J. Pulkingham and G. Ternowetsky, (eds.), *Remaking Canadian Social Policy: Social Security in the Late 1990s*. Halifax: Fernwood Publishing.

Baum, Daniel J. 1977. *Warehouses for Death: The Nursing Home Industry*. Don Mills, Ontario: Burns & MacEachern.

B.C. Politics and Policy. 1989. "Seniors becoming increasingly important political target." *B.C. Politics and Policy* 3(8):16.

Bégin, Monique. 1988. *Medicare: Canada's Right to Health*. Montreal: Optimum Publishing International (1984) Inc.

Bergob, Michael J. 1995. "Destination preferences and motives of senior and non-senior inner-provincial migrants in Canada." *Canadian Studies in Population* 22:31-47.

Black, Charlyn, Noralou Roos, Betty Havens and Leonard MacWilliam. 1995. "Rising use of physician services by the elderly: The contribution of morbidity." *Canadian Journal on Aging* 14(2):225-244.

British Columbia Premier's Forum: New Opportunities for Working and Living. 1994. *Toward Retirement: Social Safety Net Issues for Older Adults*. Background paper #4, New Opportunities for Working and Living. Victoria: Government of British Columbia.

British Columbia Task Force on Issues of Concern to Seniors. 1989. *Toward a Better Age: Strategies for Improving the Lives of Senior British Columbians.* Victoria: Ministry of Health.

Burbidge, John B. 1996. "Public pensions in Canada." In J. B. Burbidge, J. Cutt, P. Dickinson, N. Lam, M. J. Prince, C. Ragan and W. B. P. Robson, (eds.). *When We're 65: Reforming Canada's Retirement Income System.* Toronto: C. D. Howe Institute.

Burke, Mary Anne. 1994. "Interregional migration of the Canadian population." In F. Trovato and C. F. Grindstaff, (eds.), *Perspectives on Canada's Population: An Introduction to Concepts and Issues.* Toronto: Oxford University Press.

Butzelaar, F. 1991. "The retirement industry in British Columbia: An economic analysis." Unpublished paper. Available from the Centre on Aging at the University of Victoria.

Callahan, Daniel. 1987. *Setting Limits: Medical Goals in an Aging Society.* New York: Simon and Schuster.

Canadian Intergovernmental Conference Secretariat. 1998. *F/P/T Ministers Responsible for Seniors Plan for Challenges of an Aging Society.* News Release Reference: 830-595/05. Ottawa: Government of Canada.

Canadian Mortgage and Housing Corporation. 1997. *Meeting Special Needs.* Ottawa: Author. Available: http://www.cmhc-schl.gc.ca/InfoCMHC/spclneed.html

————— 1988. *Housing for Older Canadians: New Financial and Tenure Options.* Ottawa: Author.

Carrière, Yves and Louis Pelletier. 1995. "Factors underlying the institutionalization of elderly persons in Canada." *Journal of Gerontology* 50b(3):S164-S172.

Champion, Tony. 1993. "Introduction: Key population developments and their local impacts." In T. Champion, (ed.), *Population Matters: The Local Dimension.* London: Paul Chapman Publishing.

Chappell, Neena L. 1995. *Informal Caregivers to Adults in British Columbia.* Victoria: University of Victoria, Centre on Aging.

————— 1993. "Implications of shifting health care policy for caregiving in Canada." *Journal of Aging & Social Policy* 5(1/2):39-55.

————— 1987. "Canadian income & health care policy: Implications for the elderly." In V. W. Marshall, (ed.), *Aging in Canada: Social Perspectives.* Second Edition. Markham, Ontario: Fitzhenry and Whiteside.

Chappell, Neena L., Malcolm Maclure, Howard Brunt and Jennifer Hopkinson. 1997. "Seniors' views of medication reimbursement policies: Bridging research and policy at the point of policy impact." *Canadian Journal on Aging*, Canadian Public Policy Supplement:114-131.

Chappell, Neena L. and Michael J. Prince. 1994. *Social Support Among Today's Seniors.* Victoria: University of Victoria, Centre on Aging.

Chestnut, Thomas. 1993. "Using tourism to attract retirees." *Current Municipal Problems* 20:200-210.

"Consultants aim to reduce Pharmacare expenditures." 1989. *B.C. Politics and Policy* 3(7):16.

"Court rejects drug-industry challenge of BC pricing rate." 1996. *Canadian Press Newswire* June3.

Couvelier, M. L. 1990. "Budget address." *Debates of the Legislative Assembly (Hansard)* 16(1): 34th Parliament, 4th Session. Victoria: Province of British Columbia.

Cranswick, Kelly. 1997. "Canada's caregivers." *Canadian Social Trends* Winter:2-6. Also available: http//www.hc.sc.gc.ca/seniors-aines/seniors/pubs.survey.htm

Crichton, Anne, David Hsu, with Stella Tsang. 1990. *Canada's Health Care System: Its Funding and Organization.* Ottawa: Canadian Hospital Association Press.

Deller, Steven C. 1995. "Economic impact of retirement migration." *Economic Development Quarterly* 9:25-38.

Dickinson, Harley D. 1994. "The changing health-care system: Controlling costs and promoting health." In B. S. Bolaria and H. D. Dickinson, (eds.), *Health, Illness, and Health Care in Canada.* Second Edition. Toronto: Harcourt Brace.

Dickinson, Paul. 1996. "Six common misperceptions about the Canada Pension Plan." In J. B. Burbidge, J. Cutt, P. Dickinson, N. Lam, M. J. Prince, C. Ragan and W. B. P. Robson, (eds.), *When We're 65: Reforming Canada's Retirement Income System.* Toronto: C. D. Howe Institute.

Dominion Bureau of Statistics. 1936. Seventh Census of Canada, 1931. Volume 1. Summary. Ottawa: Minister of Trade and Commerce.

Doyle, Veronica M. 1989. *Provincial Housing Assistance for Low-Income Elderly Renters in British Columbia, 1979 to 1986.* Vancouver: UBC Centre for Human Settlements.

Epp, Jake. 1986. *Achieving Health For All: A Framework for Health Promotion.* Ottawa: Minister of Supply and Services Canada.

Evans, Robert G., Morris L. Barer, Clyde Hertzman, Geoffrey M. Anderson, Indra R. Pulcins and Jonathan Lomas. 1989. "The long good-buy: The great transformation of the British Columbia hospital system." *Health Services Research* 24(4):435-459.

Foot, David K., with Daniel Stoffman. 1996. *Boom, Bust and Echo: How to Profit from the Coming Demographic Shift.* Toronto: Macfarlane, Walter and Ross.

Flanagan, Thomas. 1985. *Age Discrimination in Canada.* Calgary: University of Calgary, Research Unity for Socio-Legal Studies.

Foulkes, R. G. 1973. *Health Security for British Columbians.* Volume 1. Victoria: Ministry of Health.

Gee, Ellen M. and Gloria M. Gutman. 1995. "Introduction." In E. M. Gee and G. M. Gutman, (eds.), *Rethinking Retirement.* Vancouver: Gerontology Research Centre, Simon Fraser University.

Gee, Ellen M. and McDaniel, Susan A. 1993. "Social policy for an aging society." *Journal of Canadian Studies* 28(1):139-152.

————— 1991. "Pension politics and challenges: Retirement policy implications." *Canadian Public Policy* 17(4):456-472.

Glasgow, Nina and Richard J. Reeder. 1990. "Economic and fiscal implications of nonmetropolitan retirement migration." *Journal of Applied Gerontology* 9:433-451.

Government of Canada. 1996. *The Seniors Benefit: Securing the Future.* Catalogue Number F1-23/1996-4E. Ottawa: Author.

————— 1993. *Ageing & Independence: Overview of a National Survey.* Catalogue Number H88-3/13-1993E. Ottawa: Minister of Supply & Services Canada.

Granatstein, J. L., I. M. Abella, T. W. Acheson, D. J., Bercuson, R. C. Brown and H. B. Neatby. 1990. *Nation: Canada Since Confederation*. Third Edition. Toronto: McGraw-Hill Ryerson.

Gray, Grattan. 1990. "Social policy by stealth." *Policy Options* 11(2):17-29.

Greb, Janet, Larry W. Chambers, Amiram Gafni, Ron Goeree and Roberta LaBelle. 1994. "Interprovincial comparisons of public and private sector long-term care facilities for the elderly in Canada." *Canadian Public Policy* 20(3):278-296.

Guest, Dennis. 1985. *The Emergence of Social Security in Canada*. Second Edition. Vancouver, BC: University of British Columbia Press.

Gutman, Gloria and Norman Blackie. 1986. *Aging in Place: Housing Adaptations and Options for Remaining in the Community*. Vancouver, BC: The Gerontology Research Centre, Simon Fraser University.

Harrison v. University of B.C. 1988. 2 W.W.R. 688 (B.C.C.A.).

Harrison, Trevor. 1996. "Class, citizenship, and global migration: The case of the Canadian Business Immigration Program, 1978-1992." *Canadian Public Policy* 22(1):7-23.

Health Canada. 1998. "The future of caregiving." *Seniors Info Exchange* Winter:1-16.

——————— 1996. *Seniors Guide to Federal Programs and Services*. Catalogue Number H88-3/3-1996E. Ottawa: Minister of Supply and Services Canada.

Hertzman, Clyde, Indra R. Pulcins, Morris L. Barer, Robert G. Evans, Geoffrey M. Anderson and Jonathan Lomas. 1990. "Flat on your back or back to your flat? Sources of increased hospital services utilization among the elderly in British Columbia." *Social Science & Medicine* 30(7):819-828.

Hess, Melanie. 1993. *An Overview of Canadian Social Policy*. Ottawa: Canadian Council on Social Development.

Hodge, G. 1991. "The economic impact of retirees on smaller communities: Concepts and findings from three Canadian studies." *Research on Aging* 13(1):39-54.

——————— 1989. "Retirees in the local economy: Blessing or blight?" In K. M. Cossey, (ed.), *Rural Environments and the Elderly: Impact, Contributions and Needs Fulfillment*. Sackville, New Brunswick: Mount Allison University Rural and Small Town Program.

Hollander, M. J. and P. Pallan. 1995. "The British Columbia Continuing Care system: Service delivery and resource planning." *Aging* (Milano) 7:94-107.

Human Resources Development Canada. 1998a. *Current Old Age Security Payment Rates*. April 8. [On-line]. Available: http://www.hrdc-drhc.gc.ca/isp/oas/rates_1e.shtml

——————— 1998b. *Canada Pension Plan Benefits Increase Effective January 1, 1998*. January 6. [On-line]. Available: http://www.hrdc-drhc.gc.ca/isp/news rele/9801.html

——————— 1998c. *Canada Pension Plan: Legislative Changes, April 9*. [On-line]. Available: http://www.hrdc-drhc.gc.ca/isp/cpp/cpplcqa.shtml.

Johnston, Hugh. 1996. "Native People, Settlers and Sojourners, 1871-1916." In H. Johnston, (ed.), *The Pacific Province: A History of British Columbia*. Vancouver: Douglas and McIntyre.

Joseph, A. E. and A. Martin-Mathews. 1993. "Growing old in aging communities." *Journal of Canadian Studies* 28(1):14-29.

Keating, Norah C., Janet E. Fast, Ingrid A. Connidis, Margaret Penning and Janice Keefe. 1997. "Bridging policy & research in eldercare." *Canadian Journal on Aging*, Canadian Public Policy Supplement:22-41.

Kingson, Eric R. 1996. "Ways of thinking about the long-term care of the baby-boom cohorts." *Journal of Aging and Social Policy* 7(3/4):3-23.

Labonte, Ron. 1993. *Health Promotion and Empowerment: Practice Frameworks*. Toronto: University of Toronto, Centre for Health Promotion.

Lalonde, Marc. 1973. *Working Paper on Social Security in Canada*. Ottawa: Minister of National Health & Welfare, Government of Canada.

Lam, Newman. 1993a. "Why is the CPP contribution rate going up? Looking back at the Canada Pension Plan from 1966 to 1990." In N. Lam, M. Prince and J. Cutt, (eds.), *Reforming the Public Pension System in Canada: Retrospect and Prospect*. Victoria, BC: Centre for Public Sector Studies, University of Victoria.

————— 1993b. "Fully funded versus pay-as-you-go: A projection of the Canada Pension Plan into the future." In N. Lam, M. Prince and J. Cutt, (eds.), *Reforming the Public Pension System in Canada: Retrospect and Prospect*. Victoria, BC: Centre for Public Sector Studies, University of Victoria.

Lam, Newman., Michael J. Prince and James Cutt. 1996. "Restoring the Canada Pension Plan: Stimulating the future and stimulating the social policy debate." In J. B. Burbidge, J. Cutt, P. Dickinson, N. Lam, M. J. Prince, C. Ragan and W. B. P. Robson, (eds.), *When We're 65: Reforming Canada's Retirement Income System*. Toronto: C. D. Howe Institute.

LeBlanc, L. Suzanne and Julie Ann McMullin. 1997. "Falling through the cracks: Addressing the needs of individuals between employment and retirement." *Canadian Public Policy* 23(3):289-304.

Leeson, E. A. 1995. *British Columbia's Social Safety Net*. Victoria: Government of British Columbia. [On-line]. Available: http://www.gov.bc.ca/bcben/net.html

Logino, Charles, F. Jr. 1988. "The gray peril mentality and the impact of retirement migration." *Journal of Applied Gerontology* 7:448-455.

MacDonald, Charles and Brenda-Jean Currie. 1995. "Human rights." *Canadian Encyclopedic Digest (Western)*. Third Edition. Volume 16. Title 75.

MacKenzie, Bruce. 1981. "Health care policy in B.C.: 1972-1975." In B. MacKenzie, *Health Care Policy in B.C.* Part 2. Working Papers on British Columbia Government & Politics. Victoria: University of Victoria, Political Science: B.C. Project.

Marshall, Victor W. 1997. "The generations: Contributions, conflict, equity." Ottawa: Health Canada, Division of Aging and Seniors.

————— 1995. "Rethinking retirement: Issues for the twenty-first century." In E. M. Gee and G. M. Gutman, (eds.), *Rethinking Retirement*. Vancouver: Gerontology Research Centre, Simon Fraser University.

Martin, Paul. 1996. *Budget Plan*. Ottawa: Canada Communication Group.

McDaniel, Susan A. 1997. "Intergenerational transfers, social solidarity, and social policy: Unanswered questions and policy challenges." *Canadian Journal on Aging*, Canadian Public Policy Supplement:1-21.

————— 1987. "Demographic aging as a guiding paradigm in Canada's welfare state." *Canadian Public Policy* 13:330-336.

McDonald, Lynn. 1997. "The link between social research and social policy options: Reverse retirement as a case in point." *Canadian Journal on Aging,* Canadian Public Policy Supplement:90-113.

McQuaig, Linda. 1995. *Shooting the hippo*. Toronto: Penguin Books.

Millar, W. J. 1995. "Life expectancy of Canadians." *Health Reports* 7(3):2326.

Minister of Health & Welfare. 1993. *Ageing & Independence: Overview of a National Survey*. Catalogue Number H88-3/13-193E. Ottawa: Minister of Supply & Services Canada.

Ministry of Housing, Recreation and Consumer Services. 1998. *Shelter Aid for Elderly Renters (SAFER)*. Victoria, BC: Government of British Columbia. Available: http://www.islandnet.com/~seniors/shelter.html

Ministry of Health. 1997. *Medical Services Plan: Premiums*. Victoria, BC: Government of British Columbia. [On-line]. Available: http://www.hlth.gov.bc.ca/msp/premium.html

Ministry of Health & Ministry Responsible for Seniors. 1995. *Policy Frameworks on Designated Populations*. Victoria: Government of British Columbia.

——— 1993a. *Shaping the Future of Pharmacare*. Victoria: Government of British Columbia.

——— 1993b. *New Directions for a Healthy British Columbia*. Victoria: Government of British Columbia.

——— 1991. *Closer to Home: The Report of the British Columbia Royal Commission on Health Care and Costs*. Victoria: Province of British Columbia.

Moore, Eric G., Mark W. Rosenberg, with Donald McGuinness. 1997. *Growing Old in Canada: Demographic and Geographic Perspectives*. Toronto: Statistics Canada in conjunction with ITP Nelson.

Murray, C. C. 1988. *Supportive Housing for Seniors: The Elements and Issues for a Canadian Model*. Vancouver, BC: Canadian Mortgage and Housing Corporation.

National Advisory Council on Aging. 1995a. *The NACA Position on Health Care Technology and Aging*. Catalogue Number H71-2/2-18-1995. Ottawa: Minister of Supply & Services Canada.

——— 1995b. *The NACA Position on Determining Priorities in Health Care: The Seniors' Perspective*. NACA Position Paper # 17. Ottawa: Minister of Supply and Services.

——— 1994. *The NACA Position on Community Services in Health Care for Seniors: Progress and Challenges*. Catalogue Number: H-71-2/2-16-1995. Ottawa: Minister of Supply and Services Canada.

——— 1993a. *The NACA Position on Canada's Oldest Seniors: Maintaining the Quality of their Lives*. Catalogue Number H71-2/4-1993. Ottawa: Minister of Supply and Services Canada.

——— 1993b. *The NACA Position on the Image of Aging*. Catalogue Number H71-2/2-14-1993. Ottawa: Minister of Supply and Services Canada.

National Council of Welfare. 1997. *Poverty Profile, 1995*. Catalogue Number H67-1/4-1995E. Ottawa: Minister of Supply and Services Canada.

——— 1996a. *A Guide to the Proposed Seniors Benefit*. Ottawa: Minister of Supply and Services Canada.

——— 1996b. *Improving the Canada Pension Plan*. Ottawa: Minister of Supply and Services Canada.

Northcott, Herbert C. 1997. *Aging in Alberta: Rhetoric and Reality*. Second Edition. Calgary: Detselig.

————— 1994. "Public perceptions of the population aging 'crisis'." *Canadian Public Policy* 20:66-77.

————— 1992. *Aging in Alberta: Rhetoric and Reality*. Calgary: Detselig.

————— 1988. *Changing Residence: The Geographic Mobility of Elderly Canadians*. Toronto: Butterworths.

Office for Seniors. 1998. *Information for Seniors Guide: Finances*. Victoria, BC: Ministry of Health and Ministry Responsible for Seniors. [On-line] Available: http://www.hlth.gov.bc.ca/seniors/docs/info/finances.html

————— 1995. *Information for Seniors: Your Guide to Programs and Benefits in British Columbia*. Second edition. Victoria: Ministry of Health and Ministry Responsible for Seniors.

Owram, Doug. 1996. *Born at the Right Time: A History of the Baby-Boom Generation*. Toronto: University of Toronto Press.

Prince, Michael. 1997. "Lowering the boom on the boomers: Replacing old age security with the new Seniors Benefit and reforming the Canada Pension Plan." In G. Swimmer, (ed.), *How Ottawa Spends 1997-98*. Ottawa: Carleton University Press.

————— 1993. "Historical analysis of public pension schemes in Canada." In N. Lam, M. Prince and J. Cutt, (eds.), *Reforming the Public Pension System in Canada: Retrospect and Prospect*. Victoria, BC: Centre for Public Sector Studies, University of Victoria.

Prince, Michael J. and Neena L. Chappell. 1994. *Voluntary Action by Seniors in Canada*. Victoria: University of Victoria, Centre on Aging.

Pulkingham, Jane and Gordon Ternowetsky. 1996a. "The changing landscape of social policy and the Canadian welfare state." In J. Pulkingham and G. Ternowetsky, (eds.), *Remaking Canadian Social Policy: Social Security in the Late 1990s*. Halifax: Fernwood Publishing.

————— 1996b. "Social policy choices and the agenda for change." In J. Pulkingham and G. Ternowetsky, (eds.), *Remaking Canadian Social Policy: Social Security in the Late 1990s*. Halifax: Fernwood Publishing.

Ragan, C. 1996. "A case for abolishing Tax-Deferred Saving Plans." In J. B. Burbidge, J. Cutt, P. Dickinson, N. Lam, M. J. Prince, C. Ragan and W. B. P. Robson, (eds.), *When We're 65: Reforming Canada's Retirement Income System*. Toronto: C. D. Howe Institute.

Registered Nurses Association of British Columbia. 1994. *Creating the New Health Care: A Nursing Perspective*. Vancouver: Author.

Romanow, Roy. 1996. "Renewing federalism: Why social reform is necessary." *Canadian Speeches* 10(3):23-28.

Ruggeri, G. C., R. Howard and K. Bluck. 1994. "The incidence of low income among the elderly." *Canadian Public Policy* 20(2):138-151.

"Saving the safety net." 1995. *Canadian Dimension* 29(supplement):25-32.

Schellenberg, Grant. 1996. "Diversity in retirement and the financial security of older workers." In J. Pulkingham and G. Ternowetsky, (eds.), *Remaking Canadian Social Policy: Social Security in the Late 1990s*. Halifax: Fernwood Publishing.

Seniors' Advisory Council. 1995a. *Annual Report*. Victoria: Ministry of Health and Ministry Responsible for Seniors.

————— 1995b. *Building Partnerships: Support for Informal Caregivers*. Victoria: Ministry of Health and Ministry Responsible for Seniors.

——————— 1994. *Annual Report*. Victoria: Ministry of Health and Ministry Responsible for Seniors.

——————— 1993a. *Annual Report*. Victoria: Ministry of Health and Ministry Responsible for Seniors.

——————— 1993b. *Shelter and Beyond: The Housing Needs of Seniors*. Victoria: B.C. Seniors' Advisory Council.

——————— 1992. *Annual Report*. Victoria: Ministry of Health and Ministry Responsible for Seniors.

——————— 1991. *Annual Report*. Victoria: Ministry of Health and Ministry Responsible for Seniors.

Serow, William J. 1990. "Economic implications of retirement migration." *Journal of Applied Gerontology* 9:452-463.

Serow, William J. and William H. Haas III. 1992. "Measuring the economic impact of retirement migration: The case of western North Carolina." *Journal of Applied Gerontology* 11:200-215.

Statistics Canada. 1997a. *The Nation Series*, Edition 1 (catalogue number 9350020XCB96001). 1996 Census of Canada [CD-ROM]. Ottawa: Minister of Industry.

——————— 1997b. *1996 Census of Canada – Population and Dwelling Counts. The Daily*, April 15, 1997. Catalogue number 11-001E.

——————— 1997c. *1996 Census: Immigration and Citizenship. The Daily*, November 4, 1997. Catalogue number 11-001E

——————— 1996. *Places of Birth for Total Immigrants*. More Information About Census Tables on the 1997 Internet. Available: http://www.statcan.ca/ Accessed November 5, 1997.

——————— 1994. *Population Projections for Canada, Provinces and Territories 1993-2016*. Ottawa: Minister of Industry, Science and Technology.

——————— 1993a. *1991 Census of Canada, Housing Costs and Other Characteristics of Canadian Households*. Catalogue number 93-330, Table 10. Ottawa.

——————— 1993b. *1991 Census of Canada, Labour Force Activity*. Catalogue number 93-324, Table 1. Ottawa.

——————— 1993c. *1991 Census of Canada, Selected Income Statistics*. Catalogue number 93-331, Tables 2 and 9. Ottawa.

——————— 1993d. *1991 Census of Canada, Educational Attainment and School Attendance*. Catalogue number 93-328, Table 6. Ottawa.

——————— 1992. *1991 Census of Canada, Age, Sex and Marital Status*. Catalogue number 93-310, Table 1. Ottawa.

Sutherland, Ralph W. and M. Jane Fulton. 1990. *Health Care in Canada: A Description and Analysis of Canadian Health Services*. Ottawa: The Health Group.

Taylor, Malcolm. G. 1987. "The Canadian health-care system: After Medicare." In D. Coburn, et al., (eds.), *Health and Canadian Society: Sociological Perspectives*. Second Edition. Markham, Ontario: Fitzhenry & Whiteside.

Torrence, George. M. 1987. "Socio-historical overview: The development of the Canadian health system." In D. Coburn, et al., (eds.), *Health and Canadian Society: Sociological Perspectives,* Second Edition. Markham, Ontario: Fitzhenry & Whiteside.

Townson, Monica. 1994. *The Social Contract and Seniors in Canada: Preparing for the 21st Century.* Ottawa: Ministry of Supply & Services Canada, National Advisory Council on Aging.

Weitz, H. 1992. *The Pension Promise.* Toronto: Thompson Canada.

Welch, W. Pete, Diana Verilli, Steven J. Katz and Eric Latimer. 1996. "A detailed comparison of physician services for the elderly in the United States & Canada." *Journal of the American Medical Association* 275(18):1410-1416.

Western Report. 1996. "Who's afraid of grey power? Politicians are, and their fear of seniors may derail CPP reform." *Western Report* 11(4):8-10.

Wharf Higgins, Joan. 1992. "The healthy community movement in Canada." In B. Wharf, (ed.), *Communities and Social Policy in Canada.* Toronto: McClelland & Stewart.

Wilkins, K. 1996. "Causes of death: How the sexes suffer." *Canadian Social Trends* Summer:11-17.

World Health Organization. 1986. *Ottawa Charter for Health Promotion.* Report of the International Conference on Health Promotion. Ottawa: Department of National Health and Welfare.

Zimmer, Zachary and Neena L. Chappell. 1993. "Neglected needs and emerging opportunities in seniors' markets: An argument for future research." Paper #1 in the *Community Paper Series.* Victoria: University of Victoria, Centre on Aging.